# NEW WALKS
# IN SNOWDONIA

## DON HINSON

Gwasg Carreg Gwalch

*Cover photo:*
*Llyn Gwynant from Carnedd y Cribau ridge (walk 13)*

*First edition: July 1993*
© *Don Hinson*

*Maps are based on the Ordnance Survey Outdoor Leisure Maps
for Snowdonia National Park with the permission of the
Controller of her Majesty's Stationery Office,
Crown copyright reserved.*
*Based upon the 1992 Snowdon and Conwy Valley, 1990 Harlech and Bala,
1991 Cader Idris and Dovey Forest 1:25,000 Outdoor Leisure Maps and 1986
Denbigh and Colwyn Bay 1:50,000 Landranger Map with the permission of
the Controller of Her Majesty's Stationery Office, Crown copyright.*

*ISBN: 0-86381-265-1*
*Printed and published in Wales by*
*GWASG CARREG GWALCH*
*Capel Garmon, Llanrwst, Gwynedd.*
*Tel: (0690) 710261*

## *ABOUT THE AUTHOR*

Don Hinson was a physics teacher whose chief relaxation was, and still is, walking in the country with his wife. He drew the maps and sketches for this book and she did the typing. He has also written books on physics, *Handbook of Chiltern Hill Walks, Discovering Walks in Lakeland Mountains, Walks in the Snowdonia Mountains* and *Walks in North Snowdonia.*

# CONTENTS

# LIST OF WALKS

Note: (a) many of the walks can be shortened or extended; (b) the last figure in brackets is the total height climbed. (1ft is 0.3048m.)

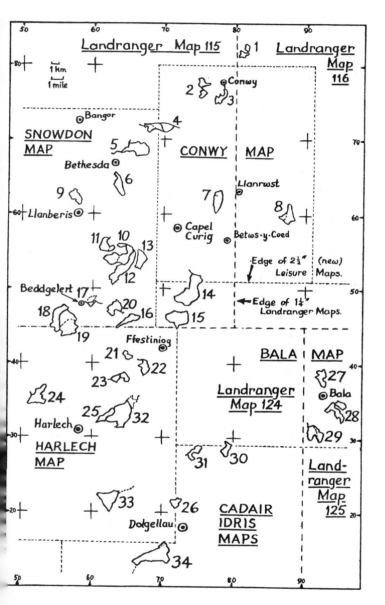

Landranger Map 115

1

Landranger
Map
116

Conwy

2

3

4

SNOWDON
MAP

Bangor

5

CONWY    MAP

Bethesda

6

9

Llanrwst

7

8

Llanberis

Capel
Curig

Betws-y-Coed

Edge of 2½" (new)
Leisure Maps.

11  10

13

12

Beddgelert  17

18

20

16

14

Edge of 1¼"
Landranger Maps.

19

15

Ffestiniog

21

22

BALA   MAP

23

24

Landranger
Map 124

27

Bala

25

32

28

Harlech

29

HARLECH
MAP

30

31

Land-
ranger
Map
125

33

26

CADAIR
IDRIS
MAPS

Dolgellau

34

1 km
1 mile

# INTRODUCTION

This book describes 34 circular walks, together with many variations. Their lengths vary from 3.5km (2¼mi) to 16km (10mi). They include 20 different walks in the popular range 5 to 8km (3 to 5mi), while those who enjoy walks over 9.5km (6mi) will also find 20 to choose from. There are walks for all kinds of walkers, from those who prefer clear paths and scenic areas to the more adventurous who enjoy the more remote regions away from it all. Some are lowland walks, some are on the lower mountains, and a few are among the high peaks.

Some of the book's special points are:

● Each walk includes little-known paths that mostly have not been described and mapped before. (More about this later.)
● Routes are chosen to reveal the natural beauty of the landscape with the minimum of difficult, tedious or unpleasant sections.
● The written route description is always beside the relevant map — not on another page.
● Route numbers on both map and written description make it easy to relate one to the other.
● The maps are accurately drawn and easily relate to Ordnance Survey maps.

The area covered consists of the Snowdonia National Park. A few of the walks are a little outside this park, but are included because of their special features. I have not explored areas south of the national grid line 320, which is just N of Dolgellau and Barmouth, except for one walk. Over 350km (220mi) of routes are described in this book.

**Walks 1 to 3** explore areas near the coast from Conwy to the Little Orme.
**Walks 4 and 5** reveal some of the lesser mountains beyond the famous Aber Falls.

**Walk 6** introduces Nant Ffrancon, the valley between the Carneddau and Glyderau mountain ranges.

**Walks 7, 9 and 21** are all chosen because of the beautiful lakes that are seen, while **walks 22 and 31** are designed to encounter impressive waterfalls.

**Walks 10 to 12** give a new look to the Snowdon range, and **walk 13** provides near views of that majestic area.

**Walks 14 to 16** reach areas where disused mines remind you of past activities without, I think, detracting much from the beauty of the terrain.

**Walks 17 to 20**, in the Beddgelert area, cover both little known small mountains and the larger and more familiar Moel Hebog.

**Walks 23 to 25 and 32, 33** include easy lowland hill walks as well as expeditions into the Rhinogydd — a range of mountains rough and rugged at the north end, but smooth in the south.

**Walks 27 to 29** introduce you to a neglected walking area near Bala.

**Walks 26, 30 and 31** are near the Afon Mawddach, also an area with potential for walking.

**Walk 34** makes a grand finale by reaching Cader Idris and its western ridge.

**In what way are these 'new' walks?**   Each walk contains, to a greater or lesser extent, paths which I have not seen adequately described or mapped elsewhere. I have consulted over 30 different Welsh walking books, but obviously there are some I have not seen. In one or two cases, better known paths have been used in order to visit waterfalls or lower mountain ridges that did not feature in my previous two books.

**Public access.**   These walks use public footpaths and, in some cases, routes where access is either a legal right or is allowed by the landowner. (E.g. mountain ridges where no fences or walls without stiles have to be crossed.) Where a public path is not waymarked, my route follows it as nearly as possible, with slight detours to avoid any obstacles.

**How to follow a route.**   A map to a scale of at least 1 inch to the mile and a compass should be taken on walks. Before using this book, get to know the words used in the walk descriptions. (See glossary below.) Note that 'up' and 'down' refer to gradients (unlike everyday speech when we go down a level road). Read the walk summary when choosing a walk to see it is likely to suit your tastes and the weather.

# GLOSSARY:

Arete: narrow rocky ridge.
Cairn: heap of stones 0.5m or more in height to mark paths, their junctions and viewpoints.
Col: the saddle shaped top of a pass.
Cwm: upper end of a valley enclosed by steep ground on three sides.
Drive: track to house or farm.
Farmgate: one wide enough for vehicles.
Lane: small surfaced road.
Leat: artificial watercourse that contours round the side of a hill.
On: keep walking in about the same direction.
Outcrop: mass of rock jutting from the ground.
Path: a way too small for vehicles.
Scramble: a steep rocky section where hands are needed as well as feet.
Scree: lots of small rocks a few inches across.
Stile: any sort of device for crossing wall, fence or hedge.
Track: a way wide enough for vehicles.

**ABBREVIATIONS**
E, N, S, W: east, north, south, west.
Km, mi: Kilometre, mile.
L: left. 'Turn L' means turn about 90°; 'half L' 45°; 'one third L' 30°; 'two thirds L' 60°; 'sharp L' 135°. 'Fork L' means take the left hand of two paths at a junction.
m: metre (roughly a yard).
P: parking off road. Free unless otherwise stated.
R: right.
●: marks a place where there is a choice of routes.

## HAZARDS AND PROBLEMS

1. Boggy patches. Wet areas have been avoided where possible, but some patches may be met. I can't promise that the ones mentioned in a walk will be the only ones you find — conditions vary from year to year.

2. The more mountainous walks should not be attempted in snow, ice or mist.

3. Since many lowland walks have rocky or rough sections, wear suitable footwear with thick soles to ensure comfort and safety.

## MAPS

The walks fall on the 1¼ inch to the mile Ordnance Survey Landranger Maps 115, 116 (only two walks on this one), 124, 125 (only three on this). The 2½ inch Outdoor Leisure Maps are optional alternatives which mark walls and fences. Over the last few years these have been reissued with slightly different boundaries. I have referred to these as the 'old' and 'new' maps when specifying which is needed for a given walk. Roughly speaking the old ones had a brown cover, and the new a yellow cover. I use the following letters for these Leisure Maps:

B - Bala; C - Conwy Valley; CI - Cader Idris; H - Harlech; S - Snowdon.

The maps in this book show details useful for following the route, but unnecessary details (e.g. stiles and walls met on a clear path) may not be drawn.

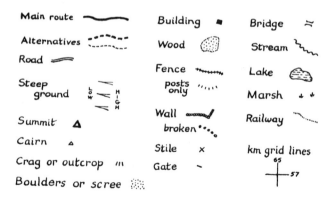

**Grid references** are given for the starting points of the walks. The first three numbers refer to the grid lines showing how far East the point is; the last three to how far North. Thus on walk 1, the number 814 means the start is 4 tenths of the way from the vertical grid line 81 to line 82, and 818 means the start is 8 tenths of the way from the horizontal line 81 to line 82.

**Buses** run near the start of some walks. Consult the timetables before using.

**Trains** stop at Blaenau Ffestiniog (walk 15), Conwy (3), Dolwyddelan (14), Llandecwyn (23), Talsarnau (24).

**Thanks.** I am grateful for the help I have had from the Snowdonia National Park regarding footpath queries, and from my wife, who typed the manuscript.

### How to see the Waterfalls
Here is a selection of the many falls of Snowdonia, with details of how to see them. Walks in my other books are given the abbreviations SM (Walks in the Snowdonia Mountains) and NS (Walks in North Snowdonia).

**Aber Falls.** Both the famous larger falls — Rhaeadr-fawr — and Rhaeadr-bach are met in NS walk 1. No book needed to reach larger one.

**Afon Cwm Llan** has a number of falls, many of which are near the Watkin Path, the largest only about a mile from the car park. See walk 12A.

**Afon Glaslyn** has one fall below Glaslyn by the Miners' Track and another near the power station (walk 12A). The latter can be visited more directly as follows: Park as for walk 13 and walk down the old road, turning R to power station. Follow the large pipe uphill. 30m before the wall blocks way, go R through gate and round wall back to pipe. Follow fence up 3 zig-zags, then bear R along path to falls.

**Blaen-pennant falls.** Some parking at the sharp bend (905 212) N of Llanymawddwy. Go along track, soon on path by fence, then back on rising track, slowly nearing the cataracts and rocky pools.

**Ceunant Mawr waterfalls, Llanberis.** NS p.96. Or go along the side road off the A4086 100m S of the Snowdon railway station, turn R under railway and L up lane. After 50m turn L along path under viaduct to reach base of falls. Scramble up for a higher view and return down lane.

**Conwy and Machno Falls.** The first is seen (for a fee) from a path starting at the Falls Café on the A5 at the junction with the Penmachno road B4406 (811 535). The second is seen 400m down the minor road north from the Penmachno Woollen Mill. View carefully on the right, opposite a house.

**Cwmorthin Falls.** There are several falls, the lowest near Tanygrisiau station. Others may be seen by going up the Stwlan Dam road to the car park (683 453) on L just before the road U-turns L. Walk up road. At the next curve L go sharp R along path under the huge tilted slab of the falls. Go L up track to see others. There is one well past Llyn Cwmorthin at 670 466 and another at the top of the rise to the old quarry. There is also much to remind you of the industrial past.

**Dolgoch Falls** is easily reached from the car park (650 047) by the B4405, SW of Abergynolwyn.

**Grey Mare's Tail.** Little known and with the unusual feature of two falls side by side. See NS walk 11, or leave the B5106 near Gwydir Castle and soon park near the junction at the top of the first rise. The falls are seen a short distance along the Llanrhychwyn road.

**Pistyll Cain and Rhaeadr Mawddach.** See walk 31.

**Pistyll Gwyn.** Park by the phone box in Llanymawddwy (903 190). The clear track starts just SW of this. Keep on over short wettish patch when track narrows. Down to ladder-stile, over stream and up to path. Follow path L, later up broad grass ridge. Enjoy the water streaming down the surprisingly long rock slab in this impressive cwm. You can get close to the top by the rough path slanting up the hillside. Up to 5km (3mi) there and back and well worth the effort.

**Porth-llwyd falls** above Dolgarrog is passed in NS walk 8B.

**Rhaeadr Cynfal** near Ffestiniog is seen in NS walk 34.

**Rhaeadr Du** near Maentwrog is reached in walk 22.

**Rhaeadr Ddu** above Ganllwyd. From the car park (727 244) go S along road and R up lane beside chapel. Fork L along path to falls.

**Rhaeadr Ogwen** is close to the A5 at the W end of Llyn Ogwen. The falls are just W of the N end of the road bridge (649 605). There is a medieval packhorse bridge under this bridge, best seen by crossing wall E of road.

**Rhaeadr-y-cwm** is seen on NS walk 35 or from near the layby (735 417) on the B4391 4km (2½mi) E of Ffestiniog.

**Swallow Falls**, N of Betws-y-coed, is reached from the A5 for a small charge, or free on NS walk 12.

**Trefriw** has impressive falls near the woollen mill. See walk 7 stages 1 and 2.

## Some notes on 'Walks in the Snowdonia Mountains'.

**Walk 9**. Elidir Fawr and Fach. There is fascinating geological exposure just S of Carnedd y Filiast, seen by going L just before the wall is met (622 626) after leaving this summit. It is a huge flat slab, tilted at a large angle, and showing a pattern of ripples dating back to the time when it once was a horizontal sandy sea shore. I first saw this on a David Attenborough TV series 'Lost Worlds, Vanished Lives'. The producer, Neil Nightingale, kindly told me how to reach the site. A rough direct pathless approach can be made by going roughly SW then SSW from where a track off the minor road in Nant Ffrancon crosses a stream at 629 639.

**Walk 20.** The return from the Snowdon Ranger path to Rhyd-ddu still poses problems. I cannot recommend the public path passing through an old quarry at 576 540. It is at first wet, pathless and tussocky, though marker posts help to guide you. The public path reaching the road at 571 536 has been diverted back to reach 568 542. Less road will be walked if you follow this revised route:

**8**   After going through gate (with ladder stile 50m to its L) watch for a faint grass track curving L after 100m. Follow the pairs of telegraph pole stumps soon with a stream on your R. **9**   At larger stream and fence, go ½R to gate. Through it and at once

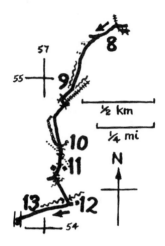

over bridge and on to cross ladder stile. Then turn R down for 50m and bear L over field, not far from its bottom wall, to far corner. **10**   Here through gate, next gate, and two gates (where railway once ran). **11**   Near farm, go through gate and bear R down track. Just after last building, go through gate and at once L through gate and over stream. Cross field to bridge. **12**   Over bridge and R along track. **13**   L along road.

## Some notes on 'Walks in North Snowdonia'

**Walk 3.**   The Great Orme. Yet another unique item of interest has appeared here — the Neolithic Copper Mine dating back to 4000 B.C., which can be visited (entry charge). Walk 3A passes the entrance which is near the top of the road to the summit.

**Walk 4A.**   Conwy Mountain. The 'quick return' from the mountain can also be made along a clear path that is parallel to the one by a wall, but nearer the ridge crest. It has rather better views.

**Walks 11, 12.**   Due to a diversion, the first sentence of walk 11 stage 3, and walk 12 stage 21 should be replaced by: At wall go over stile. Follow waymarked path, at first by wall.

**Walk 18A**   Dolwyddelan. Stage A is now way-marked and differs slightly from my route, so that you no longer cross the stream. Stage 3 should now read 'On over stile. Follow paved path'.

**Walk 26.** Aberglaslyn. Those wishing to walk from the Aberglaslyn Pass to Beddgelert and back can use a footpath on the W side of the river between the pass and the old railway bridge at 591 474, with only a short section of road to walk along near the pass.

**Walk 34, 35.** Ffestiniog. These two short walks can be joined using a scenic streamside path. At stage 10 of walk 34, cross bridge and turn L along by stream. Turn L along lane to the start of walk 35.

*Looking across the Llanberis Pass to Craig Nant Peris on walk 11.*

# 1   THE LITTLE ORME

**(6.5km, 4mi, 600ft) Map 116**

**Summary.**   After a circuit of the Little Orme with its inviting sea-cliffs, there is a further exploration of limestone country inland with a blend of open hills and natural woodland. This is an easy dry walk with just one very short steep rough section near the start. Sea birds frequent the Orme and wild flowers beautify the inland section. Being a figure-8 walk, it can, of course, be split into two shorter walks.
**Parking.**   From Llandudno turn R off the A546 at the top of the hill (just before the dual carriageway). At once fork R and park in rough layby (814 818).

**1** Go to the main road and turn L along it. **2** Turn R through small gate and R again along path. It soon rises and bears L near shrubs on its R. **3** As soon as small crag on your L is passed, fork ½L up path, soon steeply up rock, then grass. **4** Through old fence on level grass about 50m L of the highest outcrop ahead. Bear R along small path gently rising, with the outcrop on your R. **5** Follow this level path. When ground ahead drops seaward, path bears R over a low outcrop and soon there is steep grass on your L (take care). Path bears R away from sea and then runs parallel to sea but well away from the edge. **6** Near post, cross corner of an old wall and join clear path, or better walk along the crest of the small ridge L of path. **7** Make for the circular building, then turn R to walk along the top of the quarry face (carefully). Later there is a fence on your R. **8** When the path is about to enter a shrubby area, fork ½L down a path to grassy area. Follow path along edge of shrubby area. Where shrubs end, go on along clear track, soon with fence on your L. **9** On between hedges. Bear L then R through farmyard. **10** Go L along road, turn R at junction and at once fork L. **11** Soon turn R up steps. Turn R up lane and soon L along track with houses on your L. **12** 100m before group of buildings, go ½R over stile and on through small gate. When path fades bear slightly L to hedge and wall. **13** Go L along path with hedge on your R. **14** Turn R through small gate into wood. Follow path which goes on

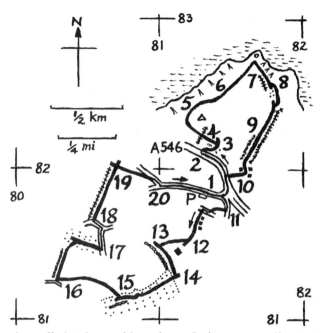

through small clearing and later bears L down to small gate. **15** Here go on by wall on your L for 50m, then turn ½R up track past two poles. You pass R of top of hill and bear gently L with track. **16** On reaching bare track go sharp R with hedge on your L. Path enters wood and bears R. **17** Turn L down lane and L along road. **18** Soon turn R over field, with fence on your L. **19** Over stile and R along path. **20** Turn R up road, soon bearing L at junction.

# 2   THE CONWY MOUNTAINS

### (9.5km, 6mi, 1300ft) Map 115, C

**Summary.**   The walk from Conwy to its mountain is deservedly well known, but from the top of Sychnant Pass it is possible to make a splendid and easy miniature mountain ramble. This reaches four summits, two of which are higher than Conwy mountain. A visit in the heather month of August makes it even more rewarding. There are fine sea and mountain views to be

*Conwy Mountain beyond a secluded pool near Sychnant Pass.*

seen much of the time and an interesting Iron Age hill fort. Paths are generally dry.
**Park** at the top of Sychnant Pass (750 770).

**1** Start walking along the track off the road (going N and seawards). Just before track bends R go on along a path that bears L, soon with steep ground on your L. It bears R to the main path. **2** Here go L up to the summit (Allt-wen). **3** Follow path that bears R with steep slope on the L. Soon turn L down path by old fence posts. Later you pass by walls on your R. **4** The path contours round a hill on your R and goes towards a larger hill. As it bears R to run between the two hills, fork L along a small path that bears L and gently rises along the side of the larger hill. **5** After crossing a scree patch the path later bears R between two large scree patches. At top of rise go sharply R up stony path that soon bears L. Make for the summit (Penmaen-bach). **6** On along the ridge path (towards Conwy Mountain). It ends at wall. **7** Here go ½R by wall and on along track. **8** Fork L down grass track. At next junction go ½L along clear stony track. Ignore three paths or tracks R of main track. **9** When track narrows to a path that bears L and gently drops with steep ground on its L, go on 20m to follow path along ridge crest. **10** Watch for a clear gap in the Hill Fort wall on your R. Keep on to explore the Fort and reach summit of Conwy Mountain, then return to the wall gap. Go down through this gap and ½L along small path. Soon turn R down path, and on along track. **11** The track narrows and bears L to join a track with wall on its L. **12** When wall goes L, go on along track which bears L past a reedy pool. **13** Over wet patch on stones L of track, then L at track junction. **14** Cross road and go through gate, with wood on your L. After wood, follow path

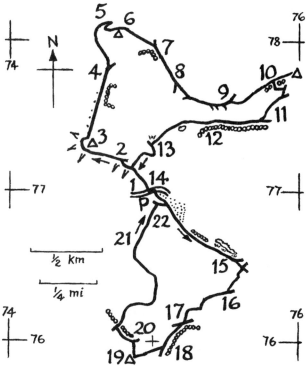

near wall on your L. **15** Soon after passing lake (just to your L)
fork R. After 30m turn R along crossing path. After 70m fork L
up path beside rushes. Soon path forks L for 5m then bears R
thus leaving rushes. **16** Turn up clear track in valley. **17** On up
near wall on your L. **18** At top of rise go ½R up path to summit
cairn of Maen Esgob. **19** Turn R along small path towards L end
of the Great Orme. **20** Turn L down track with wall on your R.
Soon go R over stile and along track. **21** After winding about for
a while the track becomes faint. Keep on down towards Great
Orme. **22** Turn R along track just before patch of rocks. Soon
sharp L.

## SHORTER WALKS
(A) Stages 1-13: 5.5km, 3½mi, 800ft;
(B) Stages 14-22: 4km, 2½mi, 500ft.

# 3  SOUTH FROM CONWY

**(9km, 5½mi, 800ft) Map 115, C**

**1** Walk along the road towards Conwy. Where the road starts to bear L towards the Castle, turn R through small gate at signpost. Up field and R along path at wood edge. **2** Up through swing gate by wood corner. Soon go R along grass track at signpost and ladder stile. Follow track passing just L of farm. **3** Turn R down road. **4** Go L through gate at signpost. Follow arrows R by wall, L over bridge, R (parallel to stream) to field and sharp L up field edge. Soon you join a clear path above stream. **5** Pass just R of farm, and 20m before gate near house, go ⅓R up path to tree and old wall near top of small rise. Here turn ⅔R (NW) along old wall (kept on your L). It soon bears L to a yellow post. Here follow hedge, kept on your L. **6** When hedge ends, bear slightly L, then R to follow fence and coppice kept on your R. At far corner of coppice, go on over grass to pass just L of small barn. **7** Here turn L to follow fence and turn R with it (keeping fence on your L). Arrows mark the route. **8** Fence bears R down to stile. Cross stile and keep on. **9** On over drive, now with fence on your R. At signpost, go on down path. Bear R down drive to road. **10** On along road for 200m, then sharp L along track. Fork R to buildings. **11** At gate go ½L between buildings, then turn R down track. **12** Turn L along road. **13** Keep on in the village until you reach the T-junction. Here turn L. **14** Turn R along main road and then L up drive. It bears L and then continues as a path.

**15** At field go ½L to contour round the hillside, soon on a clear path. **16** At chalets follow track bearing L and soon leave it to turn R over stream and stile. Here go ½L over grass to footpath sign. Follow surfaced path that soon bears L. **17** Here go R up path at footpath sign. After 100m bear L to footpath sign and stile. Cross it and continue near fence on your R. **18** Soon go down path and through gate. Here turn ½L gently up field. When stile is seen, go over it and slightly R down to gate near pines. **19** Through gate and ½L along path passing just R of hillock. Go L along lane. **20** Where road turn ½L, go on over stile. On over fields and three stiles. (The last stile is redundant.) **21** Over next stile (at first hidden by gorse) and another stile.

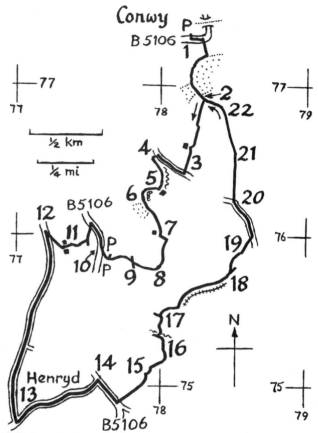

**22** Here bear L down by fence on your L. If you parked outside Conwy: turn L along grass track at stile and signpost before reaching wood; pass just L of farm; follow stage 3 etc. Otherwise return at wood the way you came.

**Summary.** Starting from Conwy, there are good views of the Castle and walls as you climb the field and enter woodland. Soon there are extensive mountain and sea views as you use paths and lanes to reach the valley in which the Afon Gyffin flows. After reaching Henryd, a quiet village, you leave the valley and follow a little known high-level path above the Afon Conwy. Finally, field paths bring you back to the wood you first met. Usually a reasonably dry walk. A few stretches are pathless, but route following is not difficult.

**Park** in the car park (not free) S of Castle by the B5106 (782 773). There is also limited parking by the entrance to Conwy Touring Park on B5106 (775 759) 2.5km (1½mi) S of Conwy. In this case the woodland section can be left out, saving you 1km (½mi) of walking.

# 4  THE FOEL-GANOL RIDGE

### (10km, 6¼mi, 1700ft) Map 115, S, C

**Summary.**  This little known ridge is a gem, with fine sea and mountain views. Its steep rough start has an easy alternative. Going on to Drum adds 4km (2½mi) and 800ft to the walk. Antiquities include the Roman road from Chester to Caernarfon; a circular enclosure ('X' on map) 35m in diameter with upright stones at nearly equal intervals, and two circular dwellings within; a circular encampment ('Y') with its foundation stones still there in the NE; some tumuli a little NW of 'Y'; a burial chamber (oval heap of stones) and two standing stones.

**Parking.**  At Abergwyngregyn on the A55, go SE along lane to Aber Falls car park near bridge (663 720). Or go to the lane end to save 3km (2mi) of walking.

**1** Walk to the lane end (ignore the R turn just over bridge). **2** To tackle the steep approach go S on a rough track. At once it does a L U-turn, but you keep on for 30m and then go L up grass track (at first vague, soon clear). This winds up. **3** On when another track is reached. Through gate. **4** Look on your R for two parallel walls and go along track until the first of these (which has probably fallen down, as it looks wiggly) points straight at you. Go on 10m and join small path at the top of a bank on your L. This runs parallel to the track, and soon bears L to pass 30m below scree patch. When a level sheep path is reached bear R along it. Then turn straight up the rough steep slope to the top.

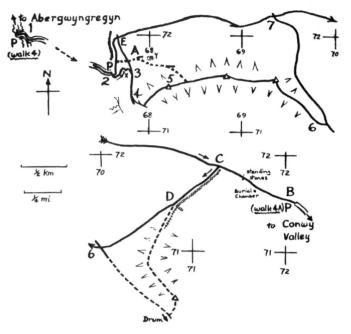

**5** Carry on along the ridge over four small summits until a track crossing the ridge is reached. (To extend the walk to Drum, go on along this track.) **6** Go sharp L down track. **7** Turn L at track junction.

**Easier ascent.**  **1** Walk to the lane end. **2** Go S on a rough track that at once U-turns L. 50m before it gets near wall turn R up grass track. On over a crossing track, now on a wide path going roughly E towards the lowest visible point of the hill. **A** Bear R off track to pass R of large walled enclosure. Follow the clear green path slanting L up the hill. At a slight fork follow the R larger rough path. On past fold to col. Here go R until you reach the top of the steep descent. Turn back and follow stages 5 to 7.

23

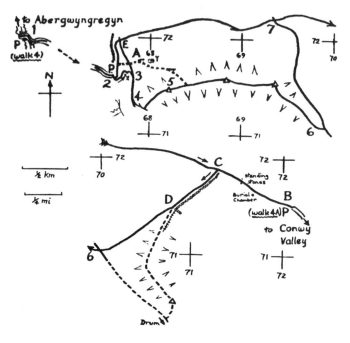

## 4A THE RIDGE FROM THE EAST

### (11km, 6¾mi, 1300ft) Map 115, S, C

**Parking.** Take the narrow road NE from Llanbedr-y-cennin, forking R after 1.5km (1mi). Then ignore turnings on the R. Park at road end (721 715).

**B** Go on along track and through gate.  **C** Here turn L up path beside wall.  **D** After passing by a wall/fence junction with stile on your L leave fence and contour round hill to col using sheep paths from time to time.  **6** At the track go on along ridge over the first grassy hill. Make for the L top of the next hill. Then bear R along the rocky ridge, soon going parallel to the stream below L. ● **5** Go carefully down the steep section and R along track. (Lower down you may find paths going R more gently down to this track.) **E** At track junction by pylons turn R.

**Easier descent.** Go back along the ridge to the first col you reach. Turn sharp L down path past fold. Pass just L of large enclosure and bear L along path. At track turn R along it. Follow stage E.

**Extension.** At point D carry on up the ridge to reach Carnedd y Ddelw, with its large ancient cairn. Then make for track. Here go R down it to col. Now follow 6. This adds 1.5km (1mi) 500ft. To follow the track L to Drum and back as well makes the whole walk 14km (8¾mi), 2100ft.

# 5   SOUTH OF ABER FALLS

### (13.5km, 8½mi, 2100ft) Map 115, S

**Summary.**   Walkers to Rhaeadr-fawr, the Aber Falls, will be impressed by the jagged outline of Bera Mawr seen well beyond it. As this peak is not on any of the main ridges it is seldom visited. It can be reached from Rachub, near Bethesda, by a route passing over the stony cone of Gyrn and crossing the attractive stream that runs down to Rhaeadr-bach, the smaller Aber Falls. Then a broad ridge takes you up to conquer the castle-like rockery of Bera Mawr. Drosgl may be visited before you drop below the 2000ft contour and return on easy paths. Views down the Aber Valley and out to sea justify the effort, while in the opposite direction the giants of the Carneddau range are set out in an impressive array. Mostly dry, except perhaps the final approach to Bera Mawr. Mostly easy walking but very rough and bouldery on the summit. In places paths are vague or absent, so some experience of map reading may be needed. Certainly not a walk to attempt when there is a chance of mist.
**Parking.** Coming from Bethesda to Rachub, fork R at the main junction bollard and at once go R up High Street. Park in layby just after no through road sign (625 680).

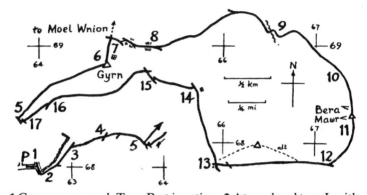

**1** Carry on up road. Turn R at junction. **2** At road end turn L with wall on your L. Follow this wall. **3** Turn ½R off track 50m before wall turns L. **4** On over crossing path. **5** At col, where path crosses to L side of pass, turn L, at first steeply up. Cross the broad grassy top, making for the stony cone ahead. **6** Here bear L (roughly N) past folds on your R, to col. (Here you can go on to Moel Wnion and back adding 1km (¾mi) and 300ft of climbing.) **7** Here turn R along track. Watch for and go to a pyramid-like rock L of track. Follow track just L of this rock for 50m to a small reed patch. Here fork L. **8** After larger reed patch, fork L at a stony area along a level path at first gently bearing L. Later it joins a clear track. **9** Track fades after crossing stream. Go L (roughly E/NE) to the crest of the broad ridge. Bear R up ridge towards the L end of rocky top. **10** At the rocks bear R and choose your own route along the boulders, bilberry and outcrops. At first there is steep ground on both sides. **11** As you leave the rocky area go SW over a flat area to Bera Bach, the next rocky area. **12** Here bear R (W) to join track on L side of hill. (Bear R off track if you wish to climb Drosgl.) **13** Ignore crossing track. Soon, at cairn, turn R along stony track. **14** Near ruin turn L down track towards the stony cone you reached at point 6. On along track that appears on your L. **15** Track bears R towards col. 100m after wet patch go ⅔L along crossing path, at first towards cone, then bearing L of it. **16** After passing under cone fork R along larger path. **17** Near col cross track and bear R to col. Follow path crossing col to L side of pass and retrace your steps.

# 6 NANT FFRANCON

**(9km, 5½mi, 900ft) Map 115, S**

**Summary.** This walk gives fine views of the mountains on either side of this valley, without involving any mountain ascents. After a short climb in the lovely woods S of Bethesda, you reach open land on the E side of the valley, with spectacular views. The gentle ascent is followed by an equally gentle descent to a point about half way along the valley. After crossing, an easy return is made down the old road and a final footpath. This has a wet patch, and if this is too bad it is not much of a detour to end the walk along the A5, which has a pavement. Stage 5 may also be marshy after rain.

**Park** in a layby just N of the turning to Ogwen Bank (637 654), which is about ½mi S of the junction between B4409 and A5.

*Nant Ffrancon.*

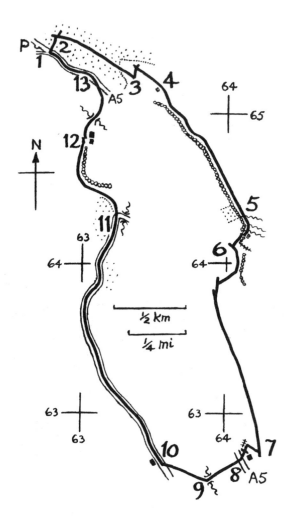

*A huge flat slab — once a sandy seashore — high above the Nant Ffrancon valley walk 6.*

**1** Go up the signposted path opposite the turning to Ogwen Bank. **2** Go through gate and turn R. After 30m fork R. **3** In the open the wide path turns sharp L. Go on towards forest, then turn R along a crossing track 80m before forest. **4** Pass fold (kept on your R) and, 100m later, fork R over grass to join path running near wall, kept on your R. **5** Above wood, cross three streams and go through wall gap to stile. Cross stile and turn L along by wall. Keep on when fence turns L. **6** On meeting grass track bear L up it. It soon bears R to stile. Here, with your back to the wall, turn ½L and walk down grass 100m to join wide grassy path. Go L down it, soon joining main path (marked by rushes and a line of stones). **7** Above farm in pines, go sharp R down path to gate. There go L (with fence on your R) over drive to small gate. **8** Over road, through small gate and on to bridge. **9** Cross bridge and go ½R over fields to farm. **10** Turn R along road. **11** As road turns R to cross river, keep on along track. Keep on down to wall and bear L to walk beside it. **12** At farm, go R through farm gate and at once L through small gate. Soon on along track. **13** Go L along pavement at road.

**Other paths.** The public path mapped through the wood (639 644) does not seem to exist. (The path I use near here is marked by arrows, indicating it can be used.)

*Llyn Geirionydd.*

# 7 LLYN GEIRIONYDD

**(7.5km, 4¾mi, 1100 ft) Map 115, C**

**Summary.** Here is a new approach to much loved Llyn Geirionydd from Trefriw, starting with impressive waterfalls. There is a short steep section which leads to an optional fine viewpoint over the Conwy Valley. The return includes a pleasant shady path through an old slate quarry, and a chance to visit the old church at Llanrhychwyn, parts built in the 12th century. It was used by Llywelyn Fawr who then ruled Gwynedd. The font may be the oldest in Britain.

**Park** opposite Trefriw Woollen Mill (784 630). Buses stop here. North Llanrwst Station is a little over 1.5km (1mi) away.

**1** From the car park turn R (N) along road and soon L up steep lane. **2** Turn L along footpath, soon beside stream. **3** After passing under bridge, turn sharp R and R to cross this bridge. At once turn R along footpath. **4** Turn R along road and L at T-junction. **5** At layby on R go R up path in wood. **6** 100m after wood at stile and just before more woodland is reached, fork ½L up small path. It becomes vague in places. Keep on gently up, and later bear L up the L side of an open strip. Make for col. **7** Over wall stile (50m before col) and on with fence on your R. (To get to viewpoint, go sharp L (E) 30m when by gate in fence. Bear R (SE) along small path. When path fades make for summit

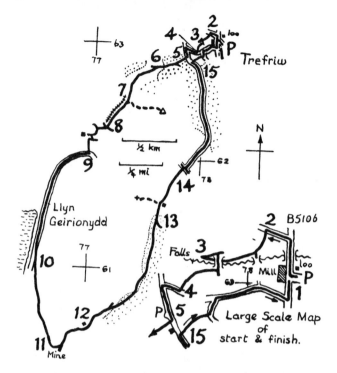

and go on a little for the view). At next gate on R keep on down small path near fence. **8** Turn ½R along track through white gate. Soon turn L along track at junction. Go L along track before reaching house, then R after 50m and L after further 50m. **9** Turn R along lane to lake. **10** At gate across road go ⅓L up path in bracken. **11** Over stile and L over level ground. Soon go L along track. On past house. **12** At next gate go on along level path parallel to forest. Leave path as it starts to rise. Make for stile and yellow arrow at wood edge. Here follow path in wood. It later leaves and re-enters the wood by stiles, before passing through mine. **13** Turn L along track. (To reach church, go L up path by house. Bear L to pass near house on your L.) Pass house (on your R) and go on along drive. **14** On along lane. **15** After the end of the forest on your R, turn ½R down path, L down lane, R at junction and L at the main road.

**Other paths.** The path N from 778 620 seems to have gone.

# 8 GWYTHERIN

**(8.5km, 5¼mi, 1000ft) Map 116, C**

**Summary.** Although this is several miles outside the National Park, I put this one in for Ellis Peters fans. St Winifred was buried here until 1137, when monks from Shrewsbury came to remove her sacred bones. This fact has been woven into one of the Brother Cadfael stories. In the churchyard beside the church there is an interesting group of four ancient upright stones arranged in a line. One has a fifth century Roman inscription. Apart from this, the beautiful valley makes splendid walking country. The walk explores both sides of the valley, giving good views of its fertile green fields and the more distant moors. It may be hard to cross the stream in stage 5 if it is in spate.

**Park** in Gwytherin near the church (876 615), reached via the B5384.

**1** Go S along the valley road. At road junction fork R uphill. **2** After more level ground is reached, turn sharp L along track. Go straight down. **3** Pass just L of house to gate and go over field, then through buildings. **4** Cross bridge and go on up track. **5** Soon after gate across track, bear L off it down bank to ruin near bottom of clear track bearing R uphill. Cross low fence just L of ruin. Cross stream and follow track up. **6** After sharp bend L, fork R up. Keep on through gate. **7** 50m after barn on R, go through gate and turn L up grass near fence on your L. By gate on L, bear R along faint track. As it fades keep on (NE) for 100m to a sort-of-gate in fence. **8** Go through to clear track and bear R along it. Soon fork R to pass through nearby gate. Later track turns L through gate and at once R. **9** Just after building on your L leave track and turn L up beside ditch. Go through gate and on (with rushes by your R) 100m to next gate. **10** Here go on NNW over grass between small hill on L and larger one on R. Soon join small path that later bears R keeping below the hill. **11** When path runs beside track, follow track through gate and on down. **12** At farm, bear R along lane back to village. **13** Here turn L twice on lanes.

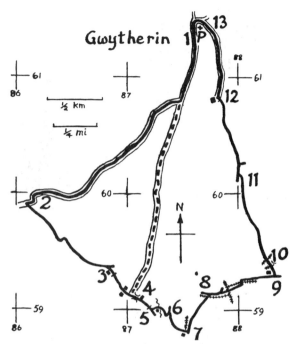

**Shorter version. (7km, 4½mi, 500ft)**  Go S along valley road to its end. Then turn L to bridge just before buildings. Follow stage 4 onwards.

**Other paths.** The footpath SSW from Gwytherin starts well but becomes hard to follow.

*The Gwytherin valley.*

*The stones in Gwytherin Churchyard.*

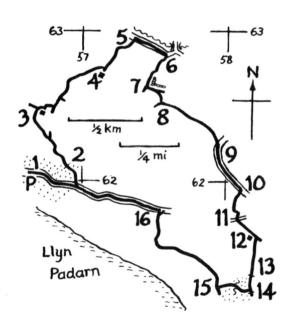

# 9 ABOVE LLYN PADARN

**(7km, 4¼mi, 900ft) Map 115, S**

**Summary.** There are many well-known walks in the woods by Llyn Padarn, but this walk is on paths over the wild open hills NW of these woods. The paths are generally good and easy to follow with fine views of the Snowdon range, Llyn Padarn, Menai Straits etc.
**Park** in the woodland car park (566 620) on the minor road just N of Llyn Padarn.

**1** Walk up the road and turn sharp L at signpost, up path in open woods. **2** On through gate into the open. Ignore path on R. Keep on, often between walls. The path later bears R. **3** Pass just L of ruins and bear R up a short steep stony path. Then go L along grass track. Soon turn L at track T-junction. **4** Turn L near house. **5** Go R along lane beside stream. **6** Before reaching road bridge, turn R along path at signpost. This bears R, then L near houses. Go through wall gap and bear R then L along path. **7** At path junction beside wall corner, turn L. Soon fork R up larger path that slowly leaves wall. **8** Through slate gate and L along track. **9** On along road. **10** Turn R down wide grass path opposite terraced houses. **11** Over road and on along surfaced track. **12** Just after Pant Gwyn, turn R down track. **13** On along path and through small iron gate. **14** Just before nature reserve entrance, turn R down path. Later path crosses two streams. **15** Turn R along track. **16** Turn L along road.

**Other paths.** Many of the public paths S of stages 3 to 8 peter out. It is easy to join the walk using the public track working E from Brynrefail at 559 626. (Follow a map; there are several junctions.) A high-level road runs SE from 548 622 to Llanberis, giving good views. It can be reached by paths going SW from the A4086 at 553 625 and 566 612.

# 10  THE LLYN LLYDAW RIDGE

**(3.5km, 2¼mi, 700ft) Map 115, S**

**Summary.** Along the N edge of Llyn Llydaw runs a perfect little nameless ridge from the car park to Bwlch Moch, which I call the Llyn Llydaw Ridge. It is an alternative approach to the Pig Track and Snowdon Horseshoe walks that nobody seems to notice, even though the start is marked on maps. It is also the basis of a fine, yet short and easy, mountain walk using the Pig Track for the return. Among the outstanding views is one along the full length of Llyn Llydaw. Some parts of the route are vague, but you are not likely to get lost in clear weather.
**Park** at Pen-y-Pass (648 556). It is only free out of season.

**1** From the car park go S along nearly level Miner's Track.
**2** Watch for a path after 200m and turn sharp R up it. It soon becomes clear and turns L. Go on over wettish patch to follow grass path (roughly W at first). At a small flat area go up path on a mini-ridge, with a larger ridge on the R. **3** When the Llanberis lakes are seen bear L on path along ridge. **4** Descend to the col using path L of ridge crest, with steep ground down on your L. Pass just R of fence to reach path junction. **5** Turn R along path.

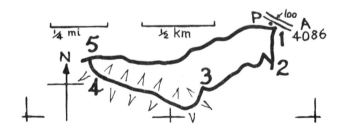

*One of the beautiful cascades on the Afon Glaslyn high on Snowdon (walk 12).*

# 11   SNOWDON FROM THE NORTH EAST

### (10km, 6¼mi, 3500ft) Map 115, S

**Summary.**   Here is a walk with much of the ascent and descent little known and unfrequented. It is every bit as tough as the famous Snowdon Horseshoe and overlaps part of that walk. It should therefore only be tackled by experienced scramblers in weather free of strong winds, ice and snow. It starts with a good path climbing beside a lovely mountain stream, which brings you to Cwm Glas Mawr. Here a flat section — almost the only part of the walk that is sometimes wettish — leads to another stream-side climb. This passes an impressive waterfall where the water pours down a large tilted rock slab. At the next flat area you turn to reach and climb the red N ridge of Crib Goch. Now follows the exceptionally fine and well known scrambly walk to Snowdon. The return is near the railway, but not for long. You soon join the ridge running N from Crib-y-ddysgl, which starts as pleasant grass, but becomes very steep, needing great care in descent. (Its a bottom-gear job!) When that final obstacle is overcome, the rest of the ridge is delightful, with a good path most of the time.

**Park.** Go down the Llanberis Pass towards Llanberis. After the bridge, park in the second (smaller) layby on the L (625 568). This is 2km (1¼mi) SE of Nant Peris car park.

**1** Go down road and sharp L along drive. Turn R to cross small bridge, go through two wall gaps and over stile. **2** Here, go on over bridge and soon L up slight path, becoming clearer later. **3** Through wall gap 50m R of stream. **4** After level section, turn L with path over stream. Make for distant stream (S/SE). (It is just R of the largest mass of rock and the L of several streams in that general direction.) If wet, use drier ground to the L. **5** Follow the R side of this stream, with path at times. **6** After passing falls the slope eases. Bear L (SE) up grass. (If you pick up a path that gets near the tilted band of white rock 8m wide and nearly 0.5m thick, go L to contour along grass and rejoin stream.) **7** Follow stream up on either side — maybe R is better. It goes up the R end of a long line of nearly level rock strata. ● **8** At top of rise, turn L along gently rising ridge. Use paths in scree to reach the L end of the red ridge. **9** Here go R up ridge. (It is exposed and has some scrambling). **10** At top, turn R along the main ridge. When it rises to a pinnacle, go along the L base of it to a small dip. Here scramble steeply up. **11** At Crib-y-ddysgl bear L to Snowdon. **12** Return down the same path. **13** At col contour to the R to go down ridge. Take great care at the steep section. Bear L to easier ground where necessary, and return to ridge later. The last fairly steep section goes down a small gully. **14** Follow path down ridge. Go sharp R with it just before a steep drop. The path fades. Go down (E) grassy ridge to join the path you came up.

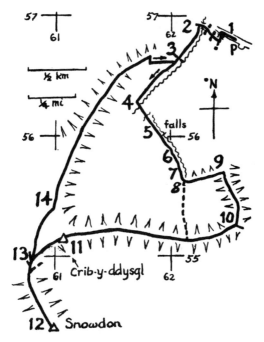

**Short cut avoiding the harder scrambles.** Follow stages 1 to 7.
**8** At top of rise note the skyline dip just R of the pinnacles. Make
for it, keeping R of marshy area. Turn R along ridge and follow
11 to 14. This saves 1km (½mi). **To avoid the very steep descent**,
either return the way you came, or at point 13 go R down the Pig
Track. (This means 2.5km (1½mi) of road walking, or a Sherpa
Bus).

**Ascent of N ridge of Crib-y-ddysgl.** Follow stages 1 to 3. When
100m above wall gap, turn ½R up grass. The ridge soon becomes
clear.

**Other routes.** At point 8, turning R down the valley gets you to
Llyn Glas. Going W from here you reach a path going L (SW) up
to Cwm Glas and Llyn Bach. Here you can climb W to gain the N
ridge of Crib-y-ddysgl (no path).

# 12 GALLT Y WENALLT AND Y LLIWEDD

## (12km, 7½mi, 2600ft) Map 115, S

**Summary.** The famous Snowdon Horseshoe walk passes over the towering cliffs of Y Lliwedd, but leaves the ridge long before Gallt y Wenallt is reached. This fine area of the Snowdon range is therefore undeservedly neglected. Here are two walks to encourage you to fill this gap. The second is quite easy, starting up one of the more attractive sections of the Watkin Path, and then following a little known but good track with views down to Llyn Gwynant. The peak is reached after a short pathless section. (Here a detour L along the ridge is worthwhile, and even Y Lliwedd can be reached without scrambling.) After a steep, but not too difficult descent, you return down the valley past the lovely Llyn Gwynant. The first walk is tough, but can be made easier and shorter. It uses the Miners' Track as far as Glaslyn. Then comes an exciting scramble — only to be attempted by experienced walkers who can cope with places like Crib Goch (though this climb is slightly easier). More scrambling over Y Lliwedd brings you to the neglected ridge — at first a miniature repeat of Y Lliwedd on the left. Just as the main path is left, there may be a wettish area before the ridge becomes drier. Descent to the valley is followed by a final path up to Pen-y-Pass.

It would be unwise to attempt these walks in mist. Any attempt to make a short cut on the descent of the second walk could lead to dangerously steep slopes, although there are ways down near the pipe-line. There may be a few wettish patches e.g. stages 15, 20, in walk 12A, the start of stage 6 in walk 12.
**Park** at Pen-y-Pass (648 556) which is often full and only free out of season, or use the Sherpa bus (which is cheaper) after parking free at Nant Peris.

**1** From car park go along nearly level Miners' Track S. **2** Near second lake fork R, soon crossing causeway. **3** Just before the third lake turn L up the ridge, first on easy ground, then a long (but not exposed) scramble. **4** At the top turn L along the path or keep on the crest for better views. Scramble up to Y Lliwedd, keeping near the L for views. **5** On down path. You may enjoy

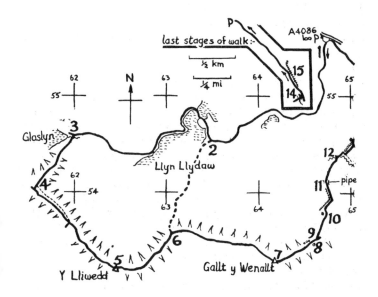

staying on the ridge crest over the third summit instead of bypassing it on the main path. **6** At large cairn where the whole of Llyn Llydaw is seen, turn ½R over grass along L edge of broad ridge. As you go on, the path becomes clearer. **7** At Gallt y Wenallt, the final summit of the ridge, follow stages 7 to 13 of walk 12A. **14** Go up the mini-ridge. Over stile and on with fence on your R. **15** 50m before fence turns R, follow path going ½L away from fence. It reaches the R corner of the car park.

### Shorter walk (9km, 5½mi, 1900ft)
**1** From car park go along nearly level Miners' Track S. **2** Near second lake fork L past building and up rough path. **6** At top of rise near large cairn, turn sharp L over grass along L edge of broad ridge. As you go on the path becomes clearer. Now follow main walk stage 7.

## 12A GALLT Y WENALLT

**(13km, 8mi, 2200ft) Map 115, S**
**Park** at Pont Bethania (628 507) on A498 5km (3mi) NE of Beddgelert.

**1** Cross the bridge and turn sharp R (N) along drive, at first near river. **2** Fork ½L up stony track. **3** After widely passing the falls, turn R down to stone slab bridge and on up by fence or wall on your L. Over stile in wall gap. Follow track until near mine. **4** Go ⅓L up path at a short stone bank 100m before track crosses stream by bridge. Over stream and up rough steps. Pass up between two ruins. Pass just R of mine waste, contouring round its base and crossing stream. **5** Now go roughly E gently up grass strip between small outcrops. Keep on L of marshy area. After route steepens keep on up grass to ridge crest. ● **6** Here turn R to summit. **7** Go on down path 60m into a mini-valley. On down narrow ridge, going carefully on the steep sections. **8** After passing ruined wall on your L, go through a wall gap and on down crest. **9** At rough stony area just on your L, go ½L off crest over old wall. Make for ruin below bracken patch. **10** Keep ruin on your L and bear L round it towards fence. Turn R beside fence and follow fence when it turns L. **11** Cross ramp over pipe. Go ⅓R up slight hill and on down towards wall. **12** Cross stream and go R down path and over stile. (Detour down to admire falls.) Turn L down small path in bracken with wall on your L. Pass ruin on your L, and another on your R. **13** Down to ruin by cables. Pass R of it, cross stream and turn L until 50m from fence ahead. Here turn sharp R up path. ● **14** Go down the mini-ridge. The path and stream soon bear L. **15** Go R over stream at wide stony patch. Join small path going gently down to run near stream. It widens to become a track. **16** 100m before power station go L over stream. (If difficult, turn R to wall corner near weather station. Here go L over low wood fence and next wire fence.) Turn R along track and through gates and on over small slab bridge. At once go L along path. **17** In field, path bears away from stream and rises to cross stile in wall. After 50m go R over second stile and L by fence. **18** Over next stile and up stony path. **19** After steps to viewpoint (with sharp drop to lake) go on down in trees. **20** Over bridge and on up field. **21** Through wide fence

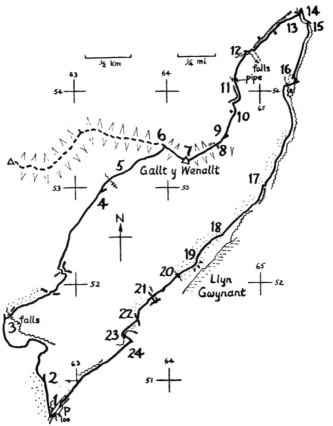

gap, then wall gap and down stony path. **22** Bear R through wall gap, soon with wall and trees just on your L. Then by grassy bank on your R. **23** Go L over bridge and bear R to stile and up to road. **24** Turn R along road.

**Extended walks.**
(1) On reaching ridge crest (point 6) turn L along ridge using paths nearest the crest. In the final stage keep R with steep crags on your R until the horseshoe path is reached. Return the same way. This adds 2km (1¼mi) and 250ft of climbing.
(2) Go L along the clear horseshoe path, soon forking R along rough path near edge. Go on to the summit and back. This adds a further 2.5km (1½mi) and 750ft of climbing.

*Snowdon, lightly snow-covered, from Carnedd y Cribau ridge.*

# 13   CARNEDD Y CRIBAU

**(8km, 5mi, 1700ft) Map 115, S**

**Summary.**   From near Pen-y-Gwryd, at the top of the beautiful valley Nant Gwynant, a little known ridge runs S to the remote Llyn Edno. From it can be enjoyed extensive views of the valley. Beyond it the wide spread of the Snowdon range will draw the eyes, especially when reflected in one of the pools that grace the ridge. The route becomes marshy S of Bwlch y Rhediad, and is not used in this walk. Instead, you descend through woods to the old road in the valley for the return. Paths are vague in the first mile, but the ridge from points 6 to 8 is fine. There may be some wettish areas. Do not attempt if misty.

**Park** 200m S of the road junction (659 555) by Pen-y-Gwryd, 6km (4mi) W of Capel Curig.

**1** Cross stile on E side of road. Go on up under wires to join a path bearing L. Soon turn R on a small path winding up the broad ridge. When it fades, keep on SSE along this ridge. **2** At top of rise, make for the point where the smooth ridge rising to L (to Moel Siabod) seems to touch the rougher ridge rising to R. With luck you may find a path going this way. **3** Cross the peat-banked

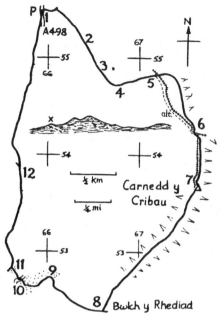

length of stream near the R end of the bank. Aim for point X in the skyline shown in drawing. Keep R of lower wetter ground. **4** On reaching greener drier grass bear L so you slant gently up the side of the ridge. **5** Bear R along by fence. This can be followed up to the fence junction (point 6), but it is better to cross at a stile and gain the ridge crest parallel to fence and about 100m from it. Rejoin the fence later on. **6** At fence junction, go R over stile, at once L over stile and R (S) beside fence. **7** Where fence turns R go ½L up path to the summit. Continue along the ridge path near old fence. **8** At the col turn R down vague path into wood. **9** Follow path in wood down to road. **10** Go L along road 20m, and R through gate. Down grass, following sunken reedy path or ditch, to trees and gate. **11** Turn R up track. **12** Ingore track forking L down to power station.

**Other paths.** You can keep on at point 8, following the fence to pass Moel Meirch and reach Llyn Edno, but there may be some extensive marshes to get through. From here the fairly dry ridge of Yr Arddu going NE, then N, takes you down to the public path going W. This section of the path is often wet.

# 14  A PENAMNEN HORSESHOE

**(16km, 9¾mi, 1900ft) Map 115, C, B**

**Summary.** The walk starts at Dolwyddelan, but soon you will be on your own by a rocky stream and then climbing to a good ridge that includes the summit of Ro-wen, with fine views towards Penmachno. After passing high above the end of Cwm Penamnen (the long valley that runs S from Dolwyddelan) you cross the peaks Foel-fras and Moel Penamnen, with new views including several upland lakes. Pen y Benar can be reached, if you wish, before the steep descent in forest and the final return along Sarn Helen, a Roman road. There can be wet patches at the S part of the walk. Suitable for an experienced walker who would like solitude and some fresh views.

**Parking.** Turn S off the A470 at Dolwyddelan and park near church.

**1** Follow road SE over railway. At the end of a line of houses on your R bear slightly R up path by footpath sign, with stream on your R. Soon after path bears away from stream, turn R up track. Follow it to the cairn on Ro-wen's summit. **2** Go on along ridge by fence on your L. At fence junction bear R, still by fence. (You may need to avoid a marshy patch near here.) **3** When near forest go L over stile. Keeping about 100m from forest, contour round to fence seen on skyline (L of forest). Soon there is a path. **4** Keep on along path when fence turns ⅔L. It may be drier nearer the forest. Follow forest edge, but short cut ½L before fence goes L then R. **5** Then go ½R to follow path 20m from fence on your R. Pass pool on your L and climb to Foel-fras. **6** Here bear L along broad ridge to Moel Penamnen. **7** Now bear R (N) along broad ridge. (Paths a bit L of crest.) **8** Over stile and on by fence for 100m, where it bends ½L. Here go R up small path to a post. Now follow path down ridge, marked by old posts. Later you walk beside grass bank. **9** At dip go R down into forest. **10** At forest bottom turn L along track (Sarn Helen).

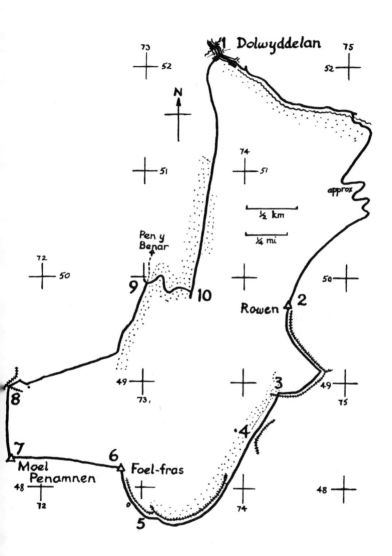

1 Dolwyddelan

73   52          75   52

N

74   51

½ km

¼ mi

approx

Pen y
Benar

72   50

9        10          50

Rowen   2

49              3       49
73,                    75

·4

8

7      6     Foel-fras

Moel
Penamnen
48
72          5

48

47

# 15  OLD MINES AND LAKES

**(10km, 6¼mi, 1100ft) Map 115, (124), B and H.**

**Summary.** Inside the National Park there is an 'island' round Blaenau Ffestinog that is excluded from park status. Even so, there is some interesting walking, with many lakes (or reservoirs) nestling in the gentle hills where you are unlikely to meet anyone. For some, the old mines will conjure up pictures of enterprises long since abandoned, while other will enjoy reaching the summit of Manod Mawr. Mainly dry paths, but some wet patches may occur in stage 11. The road at stage 9 was used to bring valuable paintings for storage inside the mountain during wartime.

**Park** (A) at main car park (702 459) in Blaenau Ffestiniog, which is not free. (B) Or drive along the road along the L (NW) edge of this car park to a T-junction and turn L and park up this quiet road (704 462).

**1** (A) If at main car park go L (SE) along main road and past crossroad. (B) If in side road, go down it and L along main road. **2** At the next small crossroad, turn L up it. Take the second turning on R. **3** At the T-junction go on up footpath. Cross stile and follow yellow marks SE. **4** Bear L beside stream to small slab bridge. Make for stile and go L up track. **5** Turn R to pass two pools. Bear R to pass Llyn y Manod. **6** Just past lake end, turn L up to a track and follow it as it slants uphill. **7** At old quarry, bear just R of huge waste tip. Go up path in slate waste which later goes down, then up again. Follow remains of poles to col. (Here you can detour SW past lake to the S summit of Manod Mawr.) **8** Go on down, bearing L to quarry. **9** When a large road goes into mountain at a gated opening, turn R. **10** Turn L through mine gates. Soon take the level middle track of a triple fork. Soon fork L along level track. **11** Turn L at track junction. (Or first explore the fascinating mine R.) **12** On reaching wide bridge over outflow from second lake on your R, turn L down path with stream on your R. **13** Up steps and L down incline. Go under bridge and follow level railway bed. **14** Turn L down incline, but leave it on L near ruin and go down track to large flat area. Look

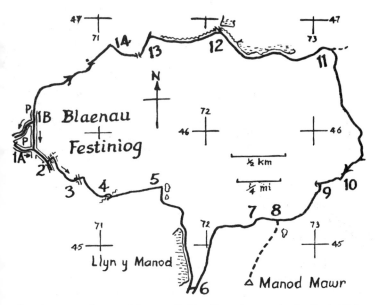

for three tracks roughly parallel in direction to the incline. Take the middle track through a row of boulders and down to the town. To reach the car park, turn R down side road.

# 16  CWM CROESOR

**(9km, 5½mi, 1200ft) Map 115 and 124, old H, or new H and new S**

**Summary.**   This walk takes you gently up the valley side to the fascinating ruins of Croesor and Rhosydd Quarries, then across the valley top to remote lakes before a splendid little-known path goes back on the other side. There is much beauty to be seen, and the limited scars that mining operations have left help you to imagine the past scene without spoiling the general outlook. Paths are generally good except for 400m of pathless progress between Rhosydd Quarry and Llynnau Diffwys, where one or two marshy areas can cause problems. Choose a dry season or a different walk if you don't like marshy ground. Don't attempt the walk in mist.

**Park** at Croesor car park (631 447).

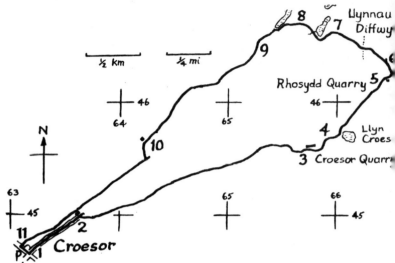

1 Turn L out of the car park and soon L along the valley road. 2 At house go ½R up track. 3 At quarry gates, go over stile and on 50m. Here take the path just behind the ruin on your R. This slants up the hill to a point directly above and beyond the far ruin (the end of a roofless building). 4 Down over the L end of Llyn Croesor and on to Rhosydd Quarry. (May be wettish near the end.) 5 Cross the slaty flat area to find a cairn 70m L of falls. Follow the slight path up. 6 Fork L at an outcrop on your R, to walk along a mini-ridge and reach a line of posts in a marshy area. Here turn ⅓R up dry grass, passing two perched blocks. Keep on to the top, thus crossing a small marsh and steeply rising to a larger marsh that can be avoided on the R. 7 Turn L to get round the L of the two lakes seen. Follow small path that runs in marshy ground for 150m near the lake edge and crosses a stream. Then go gently up (E) small rise and on down. 8 When lake is seen, bear L to cross its dam. Follow large pipe (kept on your R) down. 9 Leave pipe when clear path is reached. 10 At ruin go ½L to bridge and on to join track. 11 Go L along road.

*Llyn Dinas from near the summit of Moel y Dyniewyd.*

# 17  FROM BEDDGELERT TO MOEL Y DYNIEWYD

**(7.5km, 4¾mi, 1300ft) Map 115, new S or old H and old S.**

**Summary.**  Few people seem to know about the path that climbs SE giving a splendid bird's-eye view of the village. After visiting a minor summit or two high above Aberglaslyn, you turn along an easy heathery ridge to the rugged beauty of Bwlch-y-Sygyn and its long-deserted mine. After a short wettish stretch a good path takes you to the summit of Moel y Dyniewyd. Here Llyn Dinas and the mountains of Cnicht and the Moelwyns join the view. For much of this walk you will have already enjoyed a vast panorama, with the estuary of the Afon Glaslyn, Moel Hebog range, Nantlle ridge, Snowdon massif and Moel Siabod in clockwise turn. The return may be varied by detouring to Sygun copper mine. Route finding is easy, but mist could cause problems.

**Park** in the main car park W of Beddgelert off the A498 (588 481).

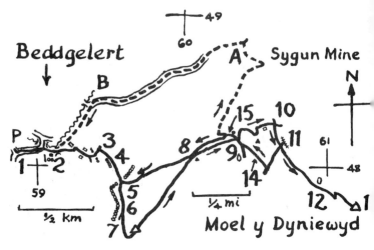

Beddgelert

Sygun Mine

Moel y Dyniewyd

**1** Walk back into village. Just before bridge turn R to walk beside river. **2** Over foot-bridge and on to R end of row of cottages. Here turn L for 50m, then R at path sign into a shrubby 'tunnel'. Go between houses and through small gate. On up steepening path. Scramble easily up rock. The path continues near R of this outcrop. Ignore small level path forking R and passing above scree. Instead fork L, soon through a small length of wall. **3** Just before path becomes level, turn R up smaller winding path. When low wall is seen to your R, keep near it until it ends. **4** Here follow path. It bears L and goes ESE and for a while is level. Note the small iron gate well ahead in wall and make for it. **5** Through this gate. (For a shorter easier walk go ⅓L along clear path to rejoin the route at point 8.) Turn R along path bearing away from wall. It rejoins wall at wall corner. **6** Here fork L up larger path to reach minor rocky top ahead. On along faint path passing just R of small pool, to next minor top. **7** Here turn L to main summit (NE 100m) on path passing just R of its top. Follow path roughly ENE along wide ridge towards a shapely small mountain. Use paths near ridge top. **8** At largish (1m) cairn, keep on along ridge. **9** On down to col. Cross the main path and on up path that bears R towards that 'shapely' peak. At top of rise it curves L and soon R to pass through mine. **10** Soon turn R along level crossing path. **11** On over next crossing path (with short length of fence on your L). Old fence posts mark your way from now on. **12** Pass pool in dip. At next slight dip follow path slanting R up hillside for 20m. It then goes sharp L 50m and sharp R now with steep ground on your R. **13** At summit cairn you could detour to explore further, or return to that 'short length of fence'. **11** Here turn L down path 200m, then go sharp R up grassy path. **14** At top of rise keep on along vague path to pass 50m R of pool and join main path. **15** 30m after going through gap in low wall fork ½L. (Or, to reach Sygun mine keep straight on, soon turning sharp R down to mine.) At path junction near cairn fork R up along path (cairned) leading back to gate at point 5. Descend the way you came up.

**Alternative return via Sygun mine. A** When path reaches level ground near mine turn L along track, soon surfaced. **B** As track turns R over bridge, keep on along path with river on your R. This adds about 1km (¾mi).

**Other paths.** The path going E, then SE, from Sygun mine seems to have gone under a forest of rhododendrons.

# 18   MOEL HEBOG

**(10.5km, 6½mi, 1900ft) Map 115 and 124, old H or new H and new S.**

**Summary.**   Here is a new route up Moel Hebog starting near Llyn Cwmystradllyn, a remote lake S of the mountain. The way is marked by many stiles and is a fairly dry ascent which gains the SW ridge without any difficulties. There are fine views of the Snowdon range and the various valleys and cwms that surround Beddgelert. After the well-known descent to Bwlch Meillionen, you follow the pleasant rocky Afon Cwm Llefrith down to the bed of an old mineral railway (there maybe a few wet patches). This gives an easy, dry return path. A fascinating slate mill ruin is passed in the car on the way.

**Parking.** From Tremadog, go W along the A487 for 3km (2mi) and fork R along a minor road. After about 1km (¾mi) turn R.

Keep on at the next junction and park near the road end by the final R turn at a house. (555 442)

**1** Walk NE along the track, passing L of the house at the road bend. Soon fork L gently up. **2** At gate in a line of trees, turn ½L up grass. Cross an old wall. Make for stile that comes into view. **3** Cross this stile and go on over two more. **4** Then go ½R to cross next stile. **5** Here go ½L to gain ridge. **6** After the summit, follow wall down to col. **7** Here turn L over stile. Follow vague paths about 50m R of a wall. Later follow the stream on your L. **8** Over stile 50m R of stream. When there is a fence beside stream, keep it between you and the stream. **9** Turn L over stile and stream and join the track bed. **10** When a wall on your L gets close, follow the track's wide U-turn. Later it becomes vague for a short distance. (If you lose the track, keep on over fields until stile gives access to road.) **11** Go L along road.

*Moel Hebog seen beyond the slate mill ruin.*

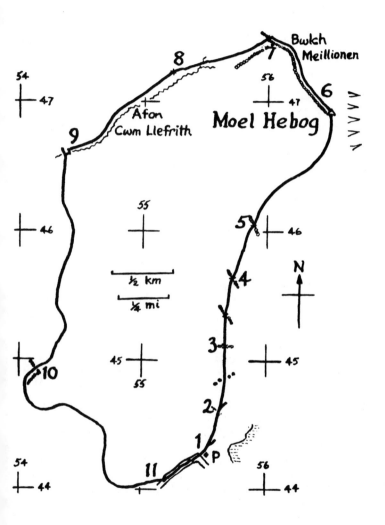

Bwlch
Meillionen

8

54
47

56
47

Afon
Cwm Llefrith

Moel Hebog

6

9

55

46

½ km

¼ mi

5
46

N

4

3

45
55

45
45

10

2

54
44

1
11

P

56
44

# 19  THE LLYN CWMYSTRADLLYN HORSESHOE

**(11.5km, 7¼mi, 2800ft) Map 115 and 124, old H or new H and new S**

**1** Go on along the road and over dam. **2** Here turn R for 100m, then L over stile and R along path (vague at first) at base of hill. **3** After 150m, path gently rises and goes through wall gap to stile by gate. **4** Here go on over field. There is a wall ahead with gate at one end and house at the other. Make for a point ⅓ of the way from gate to house. **5** Here go L up track. **6** Track ends at gate. Follow fence on your L. Go ½L through gap just after fence junction. Follow the new fence. **7** Watch for a low boulder near others flush with the ground. Here cross fence. Go on towards the junction of the wall rising up the hill on your R and the one up on your L. **8** Go through a wall gap L of the wall junction. Go slightly L up at 60° to wall until gradient eases. Then turn R up broad ridge towards the top. **9** Cross the wall where a large boulder acts as steps. Go to top and back to this wall. Follow wall (kept on your R) down through two wall gaps. Only leave wall to get round steep or wet sections. **10** Turn R over stile near col. At slight rise near pool, don't go on down into marsh. Instead, bear L along a small gently rising ridge. Make for white rocks on wall, where you cross it on stone steps. **11** Go straight up hill (NW) to wall junction. **12** Go up ridge over its S summit and on to N summit. **13** Here turn L down wettish ground to gain drier ridge going across to the final rise to Moel Hebog. Note the scree path slanting R and the grass strip on its R. **14** Pass L of the pools and go up the easier slope of a 'stream' of boulders behind pools. Fork L at more boulders and go up that grass strip. (Or bear L gently up, then go R up the scree path.) Take R forks when met. **15** Follow cairned path when slope eases. Keep on to summit. **16** Turn back down ridge, at first S, then SW. **17** At stile L of the broad ridge crest, make for the next stile seen, also L of crest. **18** Follow other stiles down to reach track near line of trees. **19** ½R along track.

**Shorter walk omitting Moel-ddu (9.5km, 6mi, 2100ft)**
**1** Walk NE along track, passing L of house at road bend. Soon

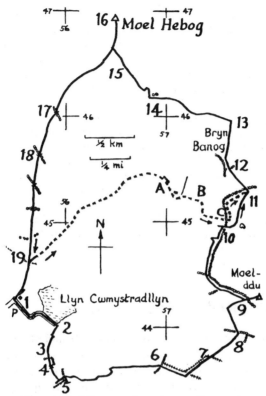

fork L gently up. **A** After overhanging wall, pass R of large ruin on track bearing L to base of incline. Here bear R between tips on wide path. Go on over a raised crossing track. Soon go on up slight path passing just L of two tips. **B** Bear R to the end of next tip and follow fading path bearing L along tip edge. At top of tip keep on up grass until wall is seen ahead. **C** Cross wall by stone steps 50m L of gate. Turn L to follow wall up, then down to cross it by stone steps. Now follow 11 to 19.

**Summary.** This walk includes the lesser known mountains S of Moel Hebog. The start is easy with views of the lake and an extensive vista of the estuary into which two rivers flow — Afon Glaslyn and Afon Dwyryd. At the end of the track rougher, mainly pathless, ground leads to the splendidly rocky top of Moel-ddu. A wall helps to guide you down to a pass and up to Bryn Banog. The descent has a few short steep sections and there could be a few wet patches. Here you can see Beddgelert and the two lakes in the valley running NE of the village. A slight wettish descent and a steep dry climb gets you to Moel Hebog. To finish, there is an easy descent down the ridge. As there are several wet areas, it is better to save this walk for drier seasons. There is a slight problem where the public path crosses a wall at 576 434, as there is no stile. At present this is solved by an easier fence crossing at point 7, where the barbed wire can be unwound and replaced afterwards. Don't attempt the walk in a mist.

**Parking** is at the same place as for walk 18.

**Other paths.** The high level route above Afon Glaslyn from 585 459 to 587 434 and W to 579 433 starts well but becomes very hard to follow. Don't try it! Also the path SW from 585 457 is there, but often wet.

# 20   YR ARDDU AND ITS LAKES

### (8km, 5mi, 1300ft) Map 115, new S or old H and old S

**Summary.**   This is an interesting walk in which each of the three small lakes way up this minor mountain are visited. First you climb the hillside to pass above the trees and turn up to gain the southern summit. After passing the first lake, a path (at times) brings you up to a sight of the other lakes and a higher summit. After visiting them, it is only a short walk to Bwlch y Battel, where you can make a diversion to the summit of Cnicht, adding 2.5km (1½mi) and 900ft. The return is down a pleasant valley with a good path beside an attractive stream, and a short stretch of road. Finally a shady path in woods brings you back. On this walk there are rough regions with no clear paths, so route-finding ability is needed, and no mist. There is one wet section at point 5, and other smaller patches.

**Park** in the car park (620 467) on the minor road 5km (3mi) S of its junction (626 503) with the A498 Nantgwynant road. (This junction is between Llyn Dinas and Llyn Gwynant.)

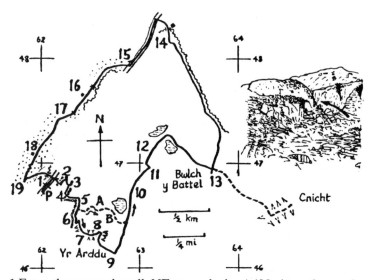

**1** From the car park walk NE towards the A498 along the road. 100m past gate across road, go R up path at signpost. Soon fork R to cross old wall near ruin. **2** On up 20m, then turn L up gently rising small path which soon bears slightly R. Turn sharp R up clear path. **3** Just as it starts a U-turn to the L, go ⅔L up small path. Soon follow wall on your L. **4** Go L over dip in wall 40m before wall junction, or L over low fence at junction. Go up hill not far from wall on your R. **5** At wet area near huge boulder, turn R with the wall, now kept near on your R. Soon cross stream. ● **6** After wall kinks L and begins to kink R at its highest point, go L up small path (NE) 40m. Then go R (SSE) along a shelf with steep ground on your R. **7** Bear L to go up bouldery gap between two outcrops (the R has a tree on it). See drawing. Soon go on (E) with larger outcrop on your R. **8** As the ground becomes level bear R to ivy patch on outcrop and R again to walk along the base of this outcrop. Bear L as this outcrop also bears L and make (roughly SE) for the summit. **9** Go down (NE) to pass just R of Llyn yr Arddu. If wet keep on higher ground to the R. **10** Follow the vague path up to the dip just R of what appears to be the highest hill. **11** Here on along path. Soon go L up gulley and R to summit. On to a second small summit. **12** Go down between the lakes and bear R onto hummock. Find the steep path down from this and go towards Cnicht (roughly SE). **13** (At

59

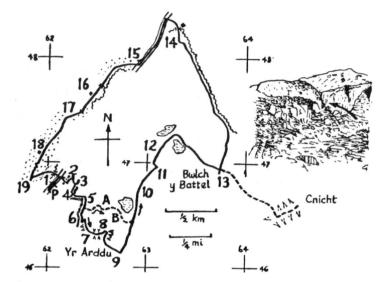

the pass you can detour on up to Cnicht: Make for the scree path just R of Cnicht — not as steep as it looks — or climb grass R of scree.) Turn L along the path down valley. **14** Over bridge and L through gate and along track. Turn L along road. **15** Soon after track on R, go ½R over stiles and follow posts across field to join path, soon with stream on your L. **16** After stile, pass just L of house. **17** Through small gate and on (at first gently up). **18** Pass just L of next house. After 100m go on up in wood, then down zig-zag path. **19** 100m after zig-zags, turn sharp L along path to bridge and road. Go R along road.

**Alternative ascent** that is easier to follow, but by-passes the southern summit. Follow stages 1 to 5 and then turn L beside stream. After 100m cross to path on L of stream. Soon cross back. **A** The path bears slightly R away from stream to get round an outcrop. It soon returns to stream. **B** At lake, bear R along path round it, keeping on higher, drier ground. Go halfway round until facing the highest summit (roughly N). Follow stages 10-19.

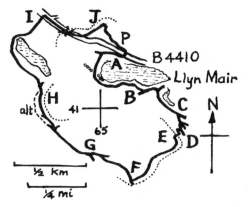

# 21   AROUND LLYN MAIR

**(5km, 3mi, 300ft) Map 124, H**

**Summary.** Lovely lakes, wonderful woodland, views of the Vale of Ffestiniog, the tortuous track of the railway, and a National Nature Reserve combine to make a memorable and easily followed outing. The woods are largely natural and are seldom dense enough to be oppresive. Most path junctions are numbered and these are shown on the map. My route is shown by letters.

**Park** in the car park near the W end of Llyn Mair, on the B4410 NW of Maentwrog.

**A** Start along the track from the picnic area, and soon turn L down path. Later it goes through a wall and at once goes L beside it. Carry on round lake. **B** On along track and soon turn R at track T-junction (11). **C** Just after second lake and falls, fork R up path (12). Soon turn R up path that at once bears L. **D** Turn sharp R at path junction. **E** Cross railway and turn L (13). Fine views. **F** Over stile and turn R (4). Later go on along track (5). **G** Keep on at junction (6) and later go on down grass path (7). (If path is wet use track on L of path to reach junction 30.) Soon fork R beside railway. **H** Go ½L over stile and up grass track (29). At junction 30 go on along track. Soon fork L to pass just L of lake. (Mountain and lake views.) **I** Turn R along road, under railway and L to station (and loo). **J** Go R through iron gate into nature reserve. Fork R down steps. Later fork R over stile and down field. (Wild flowers.)

# 22 FROM MAENTWROG TO RHAEADR DU

**(9.5km, 6mi, 800ft) Map 124, H**

**Summary.** Extensive views over the sylvan Vale of Ffestiniog are a feature of the earlier stages of this walk. After an encounter with the hydroelectric power station's pipeline, a delightful woodland path snakes up beside the tumbling stream. On the way short detours lead to spectacular sights from both the top and bottom of the falls — Rhaeadr Du. An easy track brings you back to a lane which winds back round pleasant hills and hummocks. Paths normally dry and good.

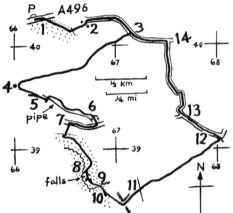

**Parking.** Going S from Maentwrog on the A496, park in layby on R (663 402), 100m past footpath sign on L at edge of wood.

**1** Go up footpath, then ⅓L through gate and past houses. **2** Turn R up road. **3** At top of rise, turn R up stony track. On through gates. **4** At cylindrical building, bear L along small path (SE) towards pipeline. It goes down to join larger path. **5** Down over stile to gate. Follow track L under pipe and at once R. **6** Fork R between houses. Soon R along road. **7** Go L over stile and down field to cross next stile. Follow path which bears R and soon U-turns L. **8** Detour R at fork to see falls and return. Ignore small L fork into pines. Take the next clear L fork into pines, but first detour R to see top of falls and return. Keep on when path joins yours from L. **9** On over stream and stile. Fork L 30m to stile at wood edge. **10** Turn R up field and L at wall gap. Go up field with fence on your L. **11** Over that pipe and on along track. **12** Go L along lane. **13** Fork R. **14** Bear L at next road junction. Return the way you came.

**Other paths** inside the area of this walk are hard to follow. A bridge is missing at 679 395.

# 23  LLANDECWYN LAKES

**(9km, 5½mi, 900ft) Map 124, H**

**Summary.**  A short and view-ful climb out of the village brings you to a delightful lake in a sylvan setting not far from habitation. This is Llyn Tecwyn Isaf. A splendid vista of estuary and mountains is seen near a little church built on an ancient site. Soon the more remote Llyn Tecwyn Uchaf is reached, with Moel Tecwyn, an imposing craggy hill, rising steeply behind it. After a wide circuit of the lake involving a short stretch of forest, a good track takes you back down an attractive (though pylon infested) valley. A generally dry route except sometimes at stage 7.
**Parking.** At Llandecwyn crossroads go E a short distance and park in the quiet side road (622 376).

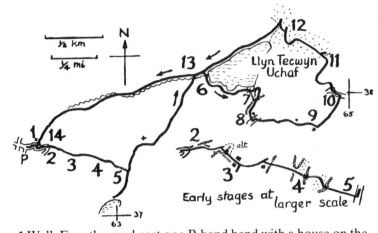

1 Walk E up the road past one R hand bend with a house on the L. At the next sharper R bend, go over stile and along by a wall (on your L). 2 Ignore gap in wall and keep on for 15m. Then go ½R up by wall. Just before a wall T-junction, go ½L along a path and soon ½R up by wall and on over stile. (If overgrown here don't go ½R, but follow path to fence gap then go sharp R to rejoin route.) 3 On between houses to track. Bear L with track. After a barn on your R bear R off track to small gate. Go through, and down slight track. 4 After trees on your L, go ½L then R to gate seen ahead in trees. Over stile and on to next stile. 5 Here turn R along lane to see the lower lake. Retrace steps along lane past church to the upper lake. ● 6 Turn R along lakeside path. 7 Over stile in wall. Soon cross stream and marshy patch, then go R along small path on L of stream. Bear R round edge of marsh to dip in wall. Cross the low wall and bear R (keeping fairly near wall) to reach clear path. Go L along this, with wall on your R. Go on through gate in fence. 8 Turn L along road. Soon go ⅓R up small path at yellow marker near house. When path fades bear R to top of short length of wall. Here follow path up to a flat area. Now follow grass track. Later pass R of small barn and just L of house. 9 Here go L along track to road and L along it. 10 When road goes sharp L, go on along track. 11 Enter wood and keep on at junction. 12 After bends, fork L at track junction. Soon, at gate, turn L up grass track. 13 Just beyond end of lake, go on down valley track. 14 Turn R down road.

**Shorter walk. (5km, 3mi, 650ft)** Follow stages 1 to 5. At the upper lake, turn back and follow stages 13 and 14. An even easier route would be to use the road to reach the lower lake.

**Other paths.** I could not trace the two paths running N from 631 380 and 658 378.

*Llyn Tecwyn Isaf*

# 24 THE HILLS OF TALSARNAU

### (11km, 7mi, 1700ft) Map 124, H

**Summary.** This neglected walking area offers a splendid little ridge near the start of the walk. Then a tiny lane, accompanied by a rocky mountain stream, takes you up through the scattered houses of Eisingrug into open country. The return to the valley includes two memorable sections of high level tracks with estuary views, and some natural woodland. A steep shady climb gets you over the final ridge, leaving only a gentle descent back to the village. A walk mainly on good paths which are usually pretty dry. Stages 9 to 15, however need care in following the route. The easier walk avoids this section. Trains stop near the start of the walk.

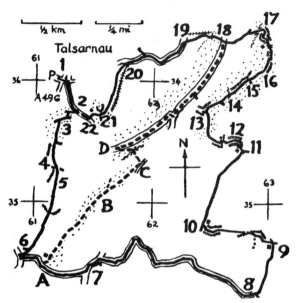

**Parking.** In Talsarnau turn W a short way off the A496 to the parking area.

**1** Go back to the A496 and on up the minor road, soon turning R at crossroads. **2** At top of rise go sharp R down path at signpost. Soon fork L up path, then go R along track. **3** After 100m, fork L up surfaced drive. When drive goes L at gate, keep on with wall on your R. **4** Just before wall ahead, bear L along path between walls. It turns R to run near wall on your R. Follow main path as it bears away from wall up to crest of ridge. **5** Bear R along ridge top. Down small valley and on through gate. **6** When lane is seen, leave track and make for gate. Here turn L along lane. Soon fork L along lane. ● **7** Turn L at road T-junction. Just after drive on R, fork R up lane. **8** When lane ends keep on along track, soon bearing L. **9** At house, turn L down field through wall gap and bear R to walk near large wall running down hillside. Watch for stone steps 50m below a junction between the wall and an old fallen wall. Over steps and down vague paths near wall. Make for a patch of pines at the R end of a track. (No path, but descent is easy.) Use the grass track between walls for the final approach to

66

the track. **10** Turn R along track. **11** At Cae'n-y-bwlch (house) leave track and bear L to reach just R of house. Here turn R along small path with wall near your L. After 100m, go down L between old walls. **12** At wall gap, go through to gate just L of barn with corrugated-iron roof. Go through gate and L by wall on your L. Soon bear R towards gate in wall. Don't go through gate, but bear R to follow wall down. Soon cross stream and go down path with fence on your L. Down steps and into wood at wall gap. Zig-zag down to wide path between walls. **13** Here turn R to follow R-hand wall. Keep on when wall ends. Don't fork R up a clearer path, but keep on, following yellow arrows. **14** At arrow on tree cross low wall, go down to stream and up by wall on your L. **15** On over wall gap, still by wall on your L. After 50m, go ½R up path by arrow. Watch for next arrow on small tree near old wall. Follow this wall to clear wall gap. **16** Turn R through gap down 20m, then L down grass (later stony) track to buildings. Here go over ladder stile on R and turn L down, soon between walls. At T-junction turn R between walls. **17** Over bridge and L to road. **18** Go up path in wood. Go through gate near top and on by fence on your R. Down into a small valley, using a path which stays up on its L side. **19** Go L along lane. **20** After passing track on R cross ladder stile and walk parallel to fence on the L. Over the next stile and on with a thin line of wood on your L. After a gentle descent there is a wall on your R. **21** At wall junction go R to small gate. Go through this and the next gate. Along drive to road. **22** Go R along road.

### Shorter easier walk (7km, 4½mi, 700ft)
Follow stages 1 to 6. **A** Soon after lane bends R, turn L along track past house. **B** After you meet a pine wood on your L, ignore track going down in pines. **C** At road go L along path to bridge and ½L up to road. **D** Go R along road. After road junction on R and track on R, you reach a footpath on L opposite track on R. Here follow stages 18 to 22.

**Other paths** (mostly good); SW from 631 369; S from 632 363; SW from 626 372; S from 620 367 (muddy); SW from 622 362 (wall without stile 1991); SW from 615 354.

# 25   A CIRCUIT OF MOEL GOEDOG

**(8.5km, 5¼mi, 400ft) Map 124, H**

**Summary.**   Moel Goedog has an iron-age hillfort 220m in diameter at its summit with several ramparts. Other signs of former life are a little stone circle and small standing stones. The first stages of the walk reveal the complexity of the Rhinog mountain range, with ridge after ridge in sight. After a glimpse of the hidden Llyn y Fedw, the views change and you see Harlech Castle and the coast on the return along a high-level track. This track may have one wettish section.

**Parking.**   At the minor cross-road 1.5km (1mi) SE of Harlech, go NE nearly 2km (1mi) to park on waste ground by drive on L to Merthyr (603 316).

**1** Walk NE along the road. Fork R along track. Soon fork R again. **2** At col and just before stile on R, fork L along track. It bears L. Soon fork L (NNE) along the clearer of two tracks. **3** Track starts to descend a wide valley. (Detour 30m L for view of Llyn y Fedw.) After track goes through gate and gap close to it, fork ½L along small path 70m before bottom of shallow rushy depression. It bears L and becomes clearer. **4** Ignore stile on R and follow track soon bearing L. **5** Keep on when the track is temporarily vague and perhaps wettish.

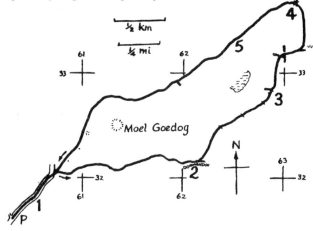

# 26  ANOTHER PRECIPICE WALK

**(5km, 3mi, 700ft) Map 124, old CI or new H and new CI**

**Summary.**   W of the well known Precipice Walk and NE of the New Precipice Walk another splendid high level path forms the basis of this enjoyable short round. Then a gentle climb uphill leads to a short stretch of forest before any easy return by lane down Cwm Wnin. The walk can be lengthened at point 8. Care is needed to follow a short section of the route (stages 5 and 6). There may be a short muddy stretch in the forest.
**Parking**. At Llanelltyd (just N of Dolgellau) on the A470, turn N up lane passing houses and derestriction signs. After ¾mi, park in layby opposite signposted track in forest on R, 716 206.

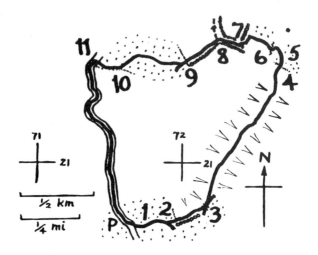

**1** Walk along the track. **2** After 250m go ½L up grass track with wall on your R. Over stile and along path, soon going down by wood. **3** At stiles turn ½L along the high level path. **4** At stile enter wood. The path soon bears L out of wood and rises until a new view is seen. **5** Go on (N) a short distance down path through two wall gaps. Note the cottage 100m to your R, but turn ½L down small path following wall on its R down to stream among trees. (If marshy, detour L to dry ground.) **6** Cross stream and go WNW on faint track just above the edge of the trees. Soon a wall is reached. Go through wall gap and turn R (still keeping above trees). At wall and fence bear L to follow wall. **7** At wall junction go through two gaps and R between two walls. Follow wall on your L through gate, over stream and up to gate. (Here you can extend the walk by going ½R along path with wall below it. Turn back when it becomes vague after ½mi.) **8** Here wall bends ½L. Follow it up, soon joining path 10m from wall. It enters forest. **9** Soon fork R along a nearly level path. **10** On reaching edge of wood follow path along edge. **11** Path veers from edge and soon reaches lane. Turn L down it.

**Other paths.** All the paths W of the lane seem to lead to dead ends.

# 27 AFON TRYWERYN

**(5.5km, 3½mi, 500ft) Map 125, B**

**Summary.** After passing through the man-made Llyn Celyn, the Afon Tryweryn bears S towards Bala. One of the few stretches of riverside path makes up the start of this walk. Then there is a climb over largely open rural country with fine views down to Llyn Tegid (Bala Lake) and the high mountains beyond, with the long stretch of the Aran range nearest. Parts of the walk go over fields without paths, but route finding is quite easy.
**Park** 200m N of the point where the A4212 crosses the Afon Tryweryn, 1km (¾mi) S of the B4501 junction. Here (913 385) park off the road where a track runs nearly parallel to the road.

**Other paths.** The path in the wood (Y Foel; 915 391) was overgrown.

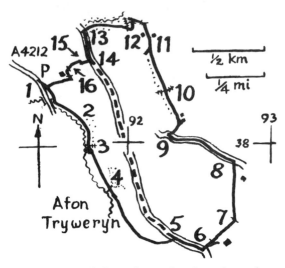

1 Go through gate and along the surfaced track nearly parallel to road. Keep on at its end, soon by river. 2 On into wood. Path rises, then sharply drops to next stile. Then it climbs again, later by a line of stones on your L. 3 At wire fence, cross it where the barbs have been removed. Cross field to distant gate. 4 Here go on along track. ● 5 Turn R along lane. 6 Turn L along farm drive for 60m, then on through gate and along grass track. 7 Well past the farm a gate is reached. Here go ½L up field, passing L of cottage and on to field corner. 8 Here turn L along lane. 9 Where lane turns L, go R along track. Soon fork L through gate and go to L of first buildings. Turn L through gate 20m before reaching barn on your L. Walk along the R side of a line of small trees. 10 Cross fence 20m R of trees, where some stones make this easier. On over field to buildings. A track is joined. 11 On past first building (kept on your R) and second (on L). Go through gate and ½L to go through next gate and down track with fence on your L. Soon L through gate and over field to end of fence on your R. 12 Here sharp R through gate and down field near trees (and stream) on the R. Soon track is joined. 13 Turn L along lane. 14 At footpath sign, turn R down field with fence on your R. 15 Go R over stile and L with fence on your L. 16 Go ½L over field to gate by farm. Through gate and L by fence. Through next gate and R along track.

An easier walk, saving 1.5km, 1mi. Follow stages 1 to 4, then turn L along lane. (Once the wood is passed, views are good.) **14** At footpath sign, turn L down field with fence on your R. Follow stage 15 and on.


# 28  CWM HIRNANT NEAR BALA

**Summary.**   These walks explore the lower end of the long deep valley along which the stream and a narrow mountain road run. Here it is possible to enjoy the open hills without spending too much time in the extensive pine forests. Paths are generally good, but you may find a few wet grassy patches. (The short cut avoids the wet patch of stage 26.)

**Walk A** starts with a fine high level track on the valley side. It then climbs in forest before reaching a wide open ridge. A pathless descent leads to a pleasant track passing by natural woods. After a short section of pine wood, the walk ends along another small open ridge.

**Walk B** passes Plas Rhiwaedog, a 17th century manor house (now a Youth Hostel) before gently climbing open fields. A forest track is followed, soon along the edge of the pines, before an enjoyable open ridge is descended. The final path descends through natural woodland.

**Park** near bridge at Rhos-y-gwaliau (944 346) a village 2.5km (1½mi) SE of Bala.

**Other paths.** Adventurous walkers will enjoy the open heathery ridge at the S end of Cwm Hirnant. Starting at Maesafallen (949 308), follow the public route (not always clear) to the forest at 936 307. Then go S/SE to Foel Goch and Foel y Geifr. Descent to the road is marshy and involves crossing a fence.

Another good route leaves the road at 952 300 and goes S up ridge. It meets a track at 954 282. Going R along this brings you back to the road at 946 273.

## (A) EAST OF RHOS-Y-GWALIAU
### (4.5km, 2¾mi, 600ft) Map 125, B

**1** After crossing bridge (from Bala) at once go L up lane (NE). **2** At manor house go on through farmyard to foothpath sign and ⅔L along track. **3** Just after gate the track forks. Here turn R to follow fence on your R. Follow fence as it bears L near gate and fence junction. **4** Carry on near bottom of wood when fence bears R. Cross small bridge at wood corner and follow fence (on your R) towards farm. **5** Through gate and go L 30m then R between buildings and up field with stream on your L. **6** At wood on L, turn L over gate and stream. Bear R through gate. Follow track, but soon fork L up grass, getting back by stream. **7** At forest corner, join track just inside forest and follow it R over stream. At larger track go on up it and on at next junction. Soon you go along forest edge. **8** Watch for stile and path sign on R (before track bears away from edge). Cross stile and continue along edge, bearing R with fence at wood corner. **9** When fence goes ½L steeply down, keep on to rejoin wood edge later. **10** At gate, go on along open track and on to stile when track turns R. Soon a wood is just on your L. **11** On over stile and field, past a marker post (near rock outcrop). At next stile follow path down. Soon it runs a little above lane, reaching it at a stile. (Other paths stay higher in the wood and become vague, but then a fence on your R leads you down to the same stile.) Go R along lane.

## (B) SOUTH OF RHOS-Y-GWALIAU
### (10km, 6¼mi, 1000ft) Map 125, B

**1** Over bridge W towards Bala and at once L up lane. **12** Go L at T-junction. On through two farms. **13** Down to two houses, then fork R up forest track. **14** Ignore grass track going down on L. **15** Ignore grass track going on. Instead, follow U-turn R. **16** After U-turn L, fork ⅔R up grassier track to forest edge. On along track. **17** 150m before it reaches forest, go R through gate and along path. When it fades, make for fence gap 150m R of forest corner. **18** Now contour L round the hill ahead to reach forest edge. **19** At forest corner, keep on 100m and L over fence. (Right of way follows edge of forest, but there was no stile, so the

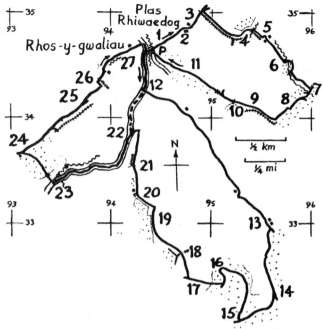

fence was crossed where it was easy to do so.) Go on down, soon with forest on your L. **20** Near lower corner, go ½R (by fence on your L) to ruins. On gently down by line of small trees on your L. On over two fields. **21** At two gates, go through the R gate, now with fence on your L. Follow track which turns sharp L to surfaced lane. (Here turn R for a quick return, saving 2.5km, 1½mi.) **22** Go L along lane. **23** 200m after track leaves stream on its R, turn R to stile into dark wood. **24** At house, turn R along track, at first near wood on R. When track goes R to gate, keep on along path with fence not far to your R. **25** At fork, take the L path gently away from fence. Path becomes vague and soon you start to descend. Watch for fence and bear L to follow it, keeping it on your R. **26** Down to gate in wall (by wet patch). Through gate to houses. Here go L over ditch and R over stile. Follow stream (on your R). When stream disappears, bear R to pass R of small barn. **27** On down field to gate and R up road.

# 29  SOUTH FROM LLANGOWER

**(11km, 6¾mi, 1500ft) Map 125, B**

**Summary.**  This walk explores the pleasant hills S of Llyn Tegid (Bala lake) without too much walking in the numerous forests of this area. At the start you climb up from the narrow gauge railway station, with views back to the lake and forward to the long high Aran ridge that stretches majestically away from you. After a partially wooded descent to the hidden valley in which the Nant Rhyd-wen flows, you take a track up this valley gently climbing its NE side. The final climb, with another fairly short stretch of forest, leads to the descent of a ridge to the valley of the Afon Glyn, and a footpath or lane back. Paths are mostly good, but can be wet in stages 16 to 18. Care is needed to follow the route in stages 12 to 18. Both these problems are dodged by the shorter walk.
**Park** by Llangower station (903 321) on the B4403 SW of Bala.

**1** Go along road towards Bala and sharp R up lane. **2** At footpath sign, keep on up grass track with stream on your L. **3** Turn R along track, through buildings and into open field. Here go ⅔L. Keep 50m R of stream, thus going through gate. **4** Over stile by gate and on along grass track. Soon ignore the track forking L up. Later there is a fence on your R. **5** When opposite gate above nearby house, go up L 50m, then R gently up faint reedy track to gate. **6** Through this gate and turn L up beside fence. **7** Through gate and turn R along small path slowly leaving fence and crossing col. **8** Down small path which bears R to reach fence by forest. Down path in gap between two forests. **9** Soon after reaching larches on your L, the path bears R away from stream and descends in trees (larches on L; pines on R). **10** Go L down forest track, later following its U-turn. ● **11** Over stream and R along road. **12** After wood, fork L at house and go sharp L to pass behind it. Head N up grass towards forest, but soon bear R before a rushy area to make for ruin. **13** Pass just R of ruin and bear R along slight track by wall on your R. After 100m, turn L for 30m up to clear track and turn L (N) along it. **14** Keep on through gate where track U-turns, and follow track (N) with wall

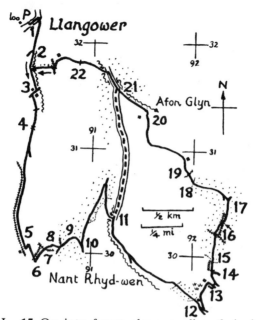

on your L. **15** On into forest along small path in heathery fire-break. On over stile. **16** Over stile on R and down dark path. **17** After path becomes more open, watch for and take another dark path forking L. Soon go on along more open grassy path. **18** On leaving forest, go down path beside old sunken track. If needed, detour R round marshy patch. Join clear track up on bank. **19** Cross stream, pass house (kept on your R) and join clear track down. **20** Near buildings, follow track bearing R then L by stream. **21** On along road and over bridge. Soon fork L to cross footbridge and turn R along path. It becomes a track. **22** After gate, go on to farm. Pass just L of buildings and go ½L up to cross stile in fence. Go on at right angles to fence, by stumps on R. Cross bridge and turn R to retrace your steps back.

**Shorter walk (7.5km, 4¾mi, 900ft)** avoiding most of the wet areas and the trickier route finding. Follow stages 1 to 10. Then go over stream and L along road. Follow stages 21 onwards. The extra stretch of road follows a lovely mountain stream.

**Other paths.** The path SE through Fedw (910 300) has gone. New forests (not on the older 2½inch map) E of this walk, make any remaining paths of little interest.

# 30   RHOBELL-Y-BIG

**(6.5km, 4mi, 1200ft) Map 124, old B, or new B and CI.**

**Summary.**  This is a short mountain excursion that visits two peaks, the larger of which is an impressive rocky cone rising out of heather-covered slopes. However, for half a mile or so after the first peak, the route is mainly pathless, with ankle-spraining ditches hidden under the heather. You start on a good path out of the valley, and when this becomes vague there is a stream to walk by. It has a beautiful waterfall cascading into a deep pool. The final climb is steeper and rockier, but without difficulties. You turn left to the second peak, Rhobell Ganol, and again L towards the tiny Foel Gron which you can visit. Near here a path gets you back to the upper sections of the Afon Mawddach, where a raised track on the far side brings you back. Extensive views all the time — a mixture of remote wild hills, extensive plantations and a sylvan valley with contrasting emerald fields and brown marshes. Not a walk for beginners or misty weather. If you arrive from the N you may like to see Llech Idris, a large standing stone W of the road (732 312) and Bedd Porius, a replica of a 5th or 6th century gravestone E of the road (733 314) not far from Pont Dôl-y-mynach, the bridge over the Afon Gain.
**Parking.**   From the road junction (769 286) near the few houses of Aber-Geirw drive E and park at the sharp bend (788 292) before the river crossing.

**1** Go on (SE) along the track at the road bend for 50m. Then go ½R up winding reedy path. Don't miss the first R turn after 100m. Ignore a small level path on R and go L up reedy path. **2** 20m before a stream ahead, fork R up small path bearing gently away from the stream. Soon go ½L along a larger path roughly parallel to stream. Soon turn R up a small grassy bank. **3** At ravine, follow the stream up. (Path at times over rough wettish ground.) **4** At wall, bear L 30m to cross it at a low gap. Make for the summit, keeping L of marshy area. **5** Turn L (SSE) carefully to the next summit, finally going up between two outcrops. **6** Turn L (NE) towards the small summit. **7** There is a slight rise near large boulder, then a descent over small stream. Go up again, keeping L of the highest point, then down to join a small

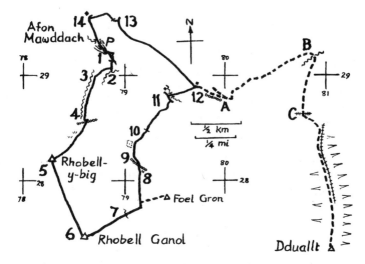

path that gently rises to pass just R of the larger outcrop, and then bears L to run N. (Leave this path if you want to visit the third peak.) **8** Soon there is a ditch on your L. When you see a wall ahead, bear L round marshy patch to join a path to gate. Go through and down path that soon bears L to second gate. **9** Go through this gate and R down track, passing just R of plantation. **10** On down through gate and gap in bank. The track winds down to a house. **11** Turn L along track. Soon go R over bridge. ● **12** Turn L along track at buildings. **13** Where track turns R, you go L 30m down to gate and R through it. Bear L to make for the farm. **14** Here go L along track to bridge.

**To visit Dduallt (adding 7km, 4½mi, 1300ft)** At point 12 go E up track on R of left hand house, soon with old wall on your R. **A** Join clear track. **B** Cross river on large stones. **C** Through gate and ½L to ridge fence. Follow this to summit, or better, keep further L for views down. Return the same way. The ridge is tussocky grass and likely to be wet, but the summit is good.

**Other paths.** The track WSW from Cwmhesgen (787 296) has gone, and the bridge at 783 294 is in a bad state. I did not see signs of the path running SE from 786 285 to 793 276.

# 31  THE UPPER AFON MAWDDACH

**(8.5km, 5¼mi, 1100ft) Map 124, CI or old B**

**Summary.**  Splendid paths high on the sides of the valley and two lovely waterfalls more than compensate for the viewless section that goes through forest. Paths are good and easy to follow, though one forest track is rough for 400m. First you descend an open path and reach the river which is followed past an old gold mine, and down to the falls — Pistyll Cain and Rhaeadr Mawddach. (These are little over a mile from the start. This is much nearer and more attractive than the usual approach from the south. Return the same way if you don't want to do the full walk.) Next you climb to enjoy a fine open view before re-entering the forest for a while. Then another climb, soon in the open, to reach a lane high along the valley. A path leads down to a bridge across the fine rocky river and up the other side. The final route across fields often lacks a path, but there are plenty of landmarks to guide you.

**Parking** is in the farmyard 743 287. Leave the A470 4km (2½mi) S of Trawsfynydd village. Go E through the holiday village, keep on when another road is joined and soon fork R. Go on to the road end.

**1** Walk back along the road 130m. As soon as wet ground is passed, turn L to walk down near stream on your L. Soon path is clear. **2** Go past first bridge. View Pistyll Cain near second bridge. Return to first bridge, detouring R for glimpses of Rhaeadr Mawddach. Cross this bridge and up to track junction. (Falls can be seen near here in winter.) **3** At junction go sharp L and at once sharp R up path. **4** Over stream. Go L along track on meeting it at its U bend. Just before house on R, go sharp L up path. **5** Go L along lane to five way junction. Here go L down. **6** At house, go L round its fence to rejoin track. **7** Near barn bear R to go through gate on R of bungalow. Go R to forest track and L along it. **8** Where track widens, go ½L down rough track. **9** At stream, go on a short distance to a fork. Here fork R up wide path. **10** Leave wood at stile (just after a short wettish area). Soon cross stream, through gate and on up rising path. Soon turn R up field to gate between houses. **11** Go on to lane and L along

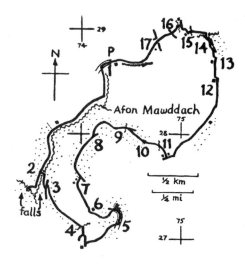

it. **12** On along track to pass just R of ruin. At once go L then R along grass track to barn. **13** Here go on down 60m and through gate. Go L 20m through wall gap and R along path with wall (later a fence and wood) on your R. **14** Through small gate just before fence turns R. Over bridge and go L. **15** Over stream and soon R at ruin. **16** At next ruin go L over bridge and L up path in bracken soon bearing up R. Make for the L wall gap. (There are other wall gaps and sections of fallen wall.) Here go ½R up small path at first aiming slightly R of wall junction (near two trees). Make for wall gap on L of this junction. **17** Pass R of the larger tree along small path going SW. Later make for a barn. Then follow wall (on your L) back to farm. Use gate R of buildings to reach yard.

# 32 NORTH FROM CWM BYCHAN

**(13.5km, 8½mi, 1600ft) Map 124, H**

**Summary.** This walk explores the northern part of the Rhinog range where the mountains are not so high or rough as they are in the central region. A gentle climb out of the Cwm, with frequent glances back to the lovely Llyn Cwm Bychan, brings you near the first summit, Clip. This is reached by a short steep climb, followed by a fine ridge walk to the start of a splendid return track. If you are energetic you can extend the walk to visit the shapely Moel Ysgyfarnogod and Foel Penolau with its impressive ramparts — a long curved outcrop of crags. Good tracks get you within 2km of the starting point, leaving only a pleasant descending path to a house and the final track. A strange circle of tilted stones — Bryn Cader Faner — may also be seen by another detour adding 2km (1¼mi) to the walk.

This is a splendid mountain walk for those used to such walking. The return is easy but quite long, so you might prefer to go back the way you came. Mostly dry, but a few (mainly small) wet patches. Do not attempt it in mist.

**Park** in the Cwm Bychan car park (644 314, not free) or at the road bend (631 314) soon after the long stretch of wood ends on the L.

**1** Walk on (E) along the road. **2** At road end, turn L over ladder stile. Go up vague path soon bearing L to run parallel to road. **3** Soon, at top of a small rise, turn R (NE) up a mini-ridge. Watch for arrow on stone and join path 15m L of it. Go up to arrow by wall gap. **4** On along clear path. **5** Follow an indistinct L fork. If this is missed a 'walking man' post will be seen 15m to your L, marking the better path. At a 'stream' of boulders on the L, which starts just R of a short length of wall, you can scramble directly to Clip up the boulders. At their top, a path goes L to a short scramble and the summit. (If this is too daunting, carry on along path 400m to cross low wall and turn L up path through wall to col. Then L again along the L edge of the ridge to a short scramble and the summit.) **6** Retrace your steps and follow path along R edge of ridge to col. (To turn back, go R down to second col and R along the path you came up.) **7** Keep on along ridge

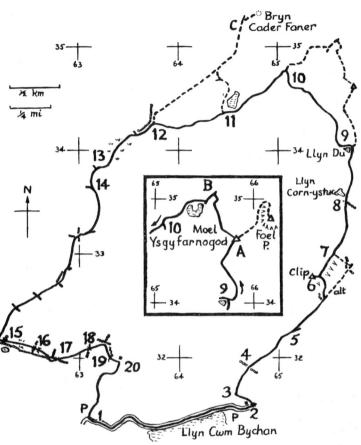

and down to wall gap near Llyn Corn-ystwc. **8** On along ridge to the R end of Llyn Du. ●**9** Here turn L along clear track. **10** Fork L at track junction. ● **11** Just after lake keep on at junction. **12** Keep on at next junction. **13** After track crosses a marshy area, keep on along grassy track when stony one turns R. **14** Over stile and L along track. It bears R, becomes faint, bears R again to join a clear track. **15** After going through several wall gaps, the track reaches a wall and bears R to run beside it. Here (near stile) turn sharp L along track to another stile. Go on past pool (on R) and between two small rocky hills (no path). On over stile. **16** After small bridge; go R to follow stream. Over wall stile and L to cross second stile. **17** Follow path bearing away from wall. **18** Over stile and on down to wall T-junction. Here turn R, soon by stream and wall to next stile. **19** Go L over stile and make for R end of house. (If wet, detour L beside wall to house.) **20** Go R along track to road.

### 32A   MOEL YSGYFARNOGOD

**(14.5km, 9mi, 1900ft)**

**Follow stages 1 to 8. 9** Here turn R along clear track. This becomes a path that contours round to the L, leading to an easy walk up the final rise to Moel Ysgyfarnogod. (Here a detour NE to Foel Penolau and back will add 1km, (¾mi). Bear L along the base of the line of crags until you reach an easy gap to ascend.) **A** Go WNW to the second (lower) top, then go N down. Llyn Dywarchen comes into view. When the slope becomes steep, move R until you can scramble down to a track near the lake. **B** Go L along the track, but soon turn R along path going round lake. Later go on along track. **10** Turn R at track junction and follow stages 11 onwards.

*Moel Ysgyfarnogod*

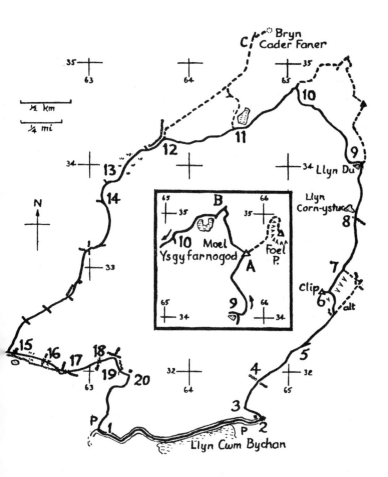

**Bryn Cader Faner:** follow stages 1 to 10. **11** Just after lake, turn sharp R along track. When track turns SE, keep on (N) to reach track and turn R along it. **C** Leave track to visit circle, then go back along track. Do not leave track. **12** At track junction with wall on R, keep on and follow stages 13 onwards.

# 33   THE LLAWLECH RIDGE

**(12km, 7½mi, 1500ft) Map 124, new H or old H and CI**

**Summary.**   After crossing the Afon Ysgethin by an old bridge, Pont Fadog, built in 1762, a gently rising track takes you past the lovely Llyn Erddyn to join the old stage coach road (London to Harlech) not far from Pont Scethin. Imagine rattling over this tiny gem of a bridge and up the steep hillside in a coach! After reaching the ridge on foot the 'road' is left and an easy descent of the long ridge begins — unless you first want to extend the walk up the ridge to Diffwys. (This adds 5.5km (3½mi) and 600ft of climbing.) On reaching a narrow pass an easy track gets you back. On the way you could make a detour to the two long burial cairns — Carneddau Hengwm. Not far from the starting point is Coetan Arthur (Arthur's Quoit), a large rock slab held up by one upright. This is another burial cairn. A straightforward walk on good paths with fine mountain and sea views.
**Parking.** Take the lane NE from the A496, ½mi N of Tal-y-bont. After winding past Cors-y-gedol between walls, turn R through a gate into open country. Park 50m before next houses (606 226).

**1** Go on along lane over bridge and up to trees. **2** Turn R with track for 50m. Then turn L along track with wall on your L. (At level area track splits. All tracks rejoin at next gate.) **3** Go on past Llyn Erddyn. Just after next gate, fork slightly L to pass through old wall and go towards the path seen well ahead. **4** At upright stone by T-junction turn R. (Or first go L to visit Pont Scethin.) The track is vague at first. It soon becomes clearer and bears L on nearing steeper ground. **5** Follow the sharp U-turn R. **6** By ancient cairn at top of rise, turn R by wall, keeping it on your L. (Or turn L up ridge if you want to extend the walk to Diffwys.) Follow wall down ridge. **7** At col turn R down path. ● **8** At bottom of steeper section, go through gate and on down to next gate. **9** Here go along clear nearly straight track back.

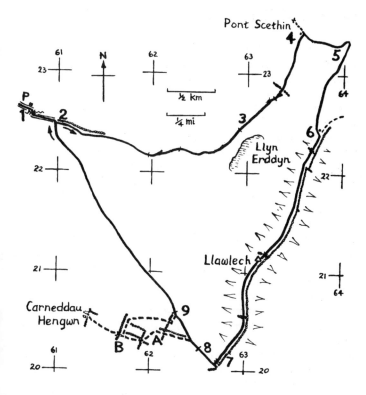

**To see Carneddau Hengwm.** After stage 7 go ½L beside wall, keeping it on your R. (No path; could be wet.) Keep on at wall T-junction. **A** Bear L to reach wall at a wall T-junction. Turn R to go 30° away from wall. Make for stile. **B** Keep on at right angles to wall. Slightly R is the end of one long cairn on your side of a wall. The rest is on the other side. Go back over stile but then turn L by wall through two wall gaps. Then turn ½R, soon on small path gently rising and bearing R over hummocky area. Later aim at a point of a wall 100m to R of ladder stile. Here, go through small gate and turn L to stile and gate. Follow stage 9. (This adds 2.5km (1½mi) to the walk.)

# 34  CADER IDRIS AND CRAIG-LAS

**(16km, 10mi, 2900ft) Map 124, CI**

**Summary.**   There are two good reasons for including this walk.
Firstly it includes the new version of the Fox's Path. I left this
route out of my first book on the Snowdonia mountains because
then it was officially described as dangerous on account of the
steep loose scree. Now the path has been re-routed and much less
scree is encountered. Secondly it gives you a chance of exploring
part of the gentle ridge that runs E, then SE from Cader Idris.
   The walk can start along a footpath to a small lily-covered
lake, but as parts of this route can be wet and boggy you may
prefer to use the road. The Fox's path is a pleasant approach to
the dominating mountains ahead. The scene is graced by much
heather, and a lake is passed before reaching the larger Llyn y
Gadair. This is a worthwhile walk in itself, if you don't fancy the
steep climb that follows. The new path ascends a rocky ridge
before turning to the main summit. It is a simple matter to visit
another peak — Cyfrwy — by a spectacular path circling high
above Llyn y Gadair. Then you descend to traverse the Craig-las
ridge. This broad ridge soon narrows and gives fine views to the
N, with Llynnau Cregennen below you, and the estuary of the
Afon Mawddach beyond. After the descent, a quiet road leads
you back. More than half of this road has a comfortable grass
verge to walk on. There maybe some wet patches here and there
(stages 1-2, 6, 17-18).
**Park** at car park (698 153), 4km (2½mi) SW of Dolgellau.

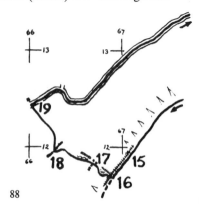

**1** Unless using the road alternative, go along the farm track beside the car park. Through gate then R over grass with stream, then wall, nearby on your R. Follow stiles and markers. **2** At lake, go sharp R along small path in rushes and over small bridges. Go up to stile. **3** Here turn L along road. Soon turn R through small gate opposite house. **4** When path becomes level fork L, thus bearing away from wall. Soon another wall appears on your R. **5** Down beside wall and up, thus leaving wall. **6** On through gate. **7** Bear R through wall gap. Soon bear R over stream, with lake on your L. **8** After a rise to the second lake, take paths towards the L end of the mountain, where a path paler than the surrounding rocks can be seen. **9** After steep scree, follow the gritty paths. Keep to L to enjoy views steeply down. It finally bears R to cairn at top of rise, and on to summit. **10** Here go on along cairned rough path. **11** Leave path, keeping near steep ground on your R, to visit Cyfrwy. **12** Follow cairns down or bear L to join main path. **13** Go through large gate. Soon leave

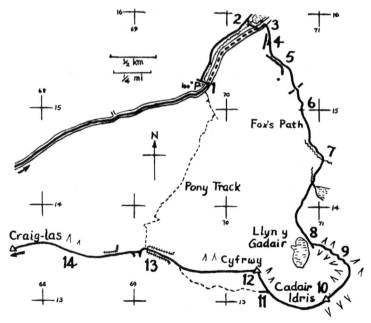

*Looking down from Cyfrwy to Llyn y Gadair*
*and Fox's paths old (A) and new (B).*

track and go ½R along small path that soon joins a track going towards a fence corner. Follow tracks or paths keeping near fence on your R. **14** At top of rise cross low fence to get better views, return to path at next ladder stile. **15** Ignore stile on R at the first col. Soon go on over stile. After a slight rise, go down to next col. (Go on to next summit and return if you wish, adding a mile and 400ft of climbing.) **16** Here turn R over stile. Follow fence down to ruin, but detour L to get round rushy area. **17** Here go on over low wall. Keep L of ditch in dip, thus moving away from wall on your R. At wall, turn L beside it to gate. **18** Through gate and along track. **19** Turn R along road.

**Other walks.** The Pony Track S from the car park reaches point 13. So you can either follow stages 1 to 12 and use it for a quick return (making a walk of 10km, 6¼mi, 2500ft) or walk up it and follow stages 13 to 19 (making an easier walk of 11km, 6¾mi, 1700ft).

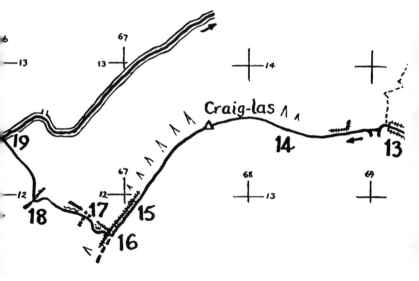

# CHECKLIST OF ITEMS
# TO TAKE ON WALKS

Rucksack with food, drink, first aid; walking boots, socks; clothes adequate for wet, cold or windy weather; map, compass; watch; money; keys. Optional: camera, binoculars, pencil, notebook.

Check the weather forecast.

For walks in more remote areas take ample food in case of delay, also torch and whistle (in case of accident).

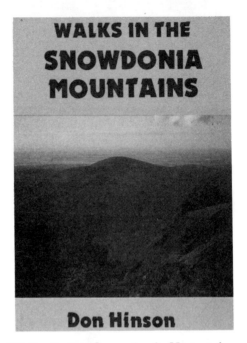

## Walks in the Snowdonia Mountains by Don Hinson

*96 pages including accurate maps and drawings;*
*ISBN: 0-86381-065-9; Price: £1.99*

Snowdonia is a splendid and wild area of North Wales noted for its rugged mountains, remote upland lakes and pools, from which tumble rocky streams and waterfalls, and its natural woods and plantations clothing the lower slopes and valleys. The best way to enjoy this beauty is by walking — many places in this area cannot be seen in any other way. Some of the walks are well known, but many are mapped and described in detail for the first time.

This book describes 45 walks, mostly circular, varying in length from 3.5 km (2¼ miles) to 16 km (10 miles).

## Walks in North Snowdonia by Don Hinson

*96 pages including accurate maps and drawings; ISBN: 0-86381-122-1; Price: £1.99*

Snowdonia is a splendid and wild area of North Wales noted for its rugged mountains, remote upland lakes and pools, from which tumble rocky streams and waterfalls, and its natural woods and plantations clothing the lower slopes and valleys. The best way to enjoy this beauty is by walking — many places in this area cannot be seen any other way. Some of the walks are well known, but many are mapped and described in detail for the first time.

Over 400 km (250 mi) of routes are mapped and described, making the book exceptionally good value for money. There are also comments on a further 100 km of paths which should help those wishing to explore the area further.